VISUALITY FOR ARCHITECTS

VISUALITY FOR

ARCHITECTS

Architectural Creativity and Modern Theories
of Perception and Imagination

BRANKO MITROVIĆ

UNIVERSITY OF VIRGINIA PRESS   CHARLOTTESVILLE AND LONDON

University of Virginia Press

First published 2013

9 8 7 6 5 4 3 2

LIBRARY OF CONGRESS CATALOGING-IN-PUBLICATION DATA

Mitrović, Branko.
  Visuality for architects : architectural creativity and modern theories of
perception and imagination / Branko Mitrović.
     pages   cm
  Includes bibliographical references and index.
  ISBN 978-0-8139-3378-8 (cloth)—ISBN 978-0-8139-3379-5(pbk)
—ISBN 978-0-8139-3396-2(e- book)
  1. Architecture—Philosophy. 2. Visual perception—Psychological aspects.
I. Title.
  NA2500.M595 2013
  720.1—dc23

                                                            2012044555

*Figures 2, 10–13, and 18 by the author. Technical preparation of figures 3–6, 15, and
16 by Carley Lockie. Technical preparation of figures 7–9 by Arnika Blount. All other
illustrations used by permission of the designer.*

In memoriam Ivek Grabovac

I urge you to open your eyes.

—LE CORBUSIER

CONTENTS

PREFACE

In 2002 I was present at the opening of an exhibition at an East Coast architectural institution. Six large exposition rooms were made available to six groups of young architects, who presented a series of visual experiments that explored combinations of spatial elements and colors. The exhibition was thoughtfully put together; the experiments consisted of surfaces in various colors combined at different angles. One could move up, down, and between multicolored planes and platforms and perceive unexpected spatial relationships of forms and colors. Having had the chance to see the exhibition before the opening, I noted that this kind of work was not aligned with the mainstream architectural production of the day. The contemporary trend was to suppress visual and formal concerns and concentrate on the stories that can be told about architectural works. I was therefore curious to hear the reaction of the prominent architectural critic whom the hosts invited to open the exhibition. I could sense that a storm was brewing.

And I was right. The critic came, dashed through the exposition rooms without much interest, and then started his talk, holding the brief two-page exhibition catalog in his hand. He was calm and his words were pronounced politely—yet his assault was damning in every possible sense. These young architects were wasting their time, he argued, because they concentrated on shapes, spaces, and colors, while architecture can only be a reflection of its social and cultural role—the important topic unmentioned in the catalog. The only way to approach architecture, he explained, is through words. One can only think in words; since everything is text, architects can only make texts. Nevertheless, these young architects had written very little in their catalog, a fact that particularly disturbed him. Ultimately, the role of the architect is that of a public intellectual and words are the only medium architects can engage in, he argued. In the little that they had written, these young architects seemed to suggest that they could engage with architecture using media that are not verbal—an absurd assumption that lacks awareness of contemporary architectural theory. This disparaging talk went on for about half an hour; its gloomy and condemning tone was in sharp contrast with the cheerful colors of the installations lurking behind the door. The people who gathered for the opening respectfully listened to the famous critic and then went to enjoy the exhibition. Everyone but the critic, I had the impression, liked it.

By that time I had worked long enough in architectural academia to be able to predict the critic's reaction. I knew that the expectation of hearing a story dominated studio reviews to the point that it often killed the critics' ability to engage with architecture's visual properties. I had seen studio reviews in which students would pin up pages of typed text on the wall, rather than drawings, because they were taught in theory classes that "everything is a text." I used to deplore the trend, but at the time I also misunderstood how it came about. My explanation in those days was that the trend originated from the tendency of architecture schools to hire those graduates who are more skillful with words than those who are confident with things visual. As a result, generation after generation, architectural academia gradually painted itself in a corner where only words mattered. As I now understand, this explanation was simplistic and wrong. The antiformalism that dominates much of architectural academia today has a complex history and diverse intellectual roots. At the time I failed to grasp this. (In fact, I doubt that even the critic I've just mentioned, who was so passionately involved in the contemporary theoretical debates of the time, was aware of the full picture of what he was preaching.) In any case, I knew that some aspects of the critic's worldview could not be right. For instance, the view that all thinking is verbal could not be true, since there existed a substantial body of psychological research on visual imagination and mental rotation—that is, thought processes independent of verbal thinking (see chap. 4 of this book). I also knew about the latest articulations of the formalist position in aesthetics by Nick Zangwill (see chap. 5). The critic who opened the exhibition would find it hard to respond to Zangwill's arguments—but few people working in architectural theory read the specialist journals on analytic aesthetics in which Zangwill's early papers were published. It was only in later years, as I came to study the important breakthroughs in the study of human visuality that have occurred in recent decades, that I also gradually became aware of the roots of the antiformalism that dominates contemporary architectural theory. In the process, I also learned that architectural antiformalism is based on philosophical and psychological assumptions that have in the meantime become obsolete in the fields they originated from. As time went by, I also gradually learned about an entire generation of young architects who embraced formalist approach to design; some of their works now illustrate this book.

Rudolf Arnheim in his *Dynamics of Architectural Form* described the formal exhilaration that he often found in architecture. At the same time, he reported how puzzled he was to observe "in the practitioners of architecture, professionals, teachers, and students, a kind of malaise, a disillusionment that made them neglect the active study of design or even denounce it as a frivolous diversion from the serious social obligations of the architect."[1] The expectation that one must justify architectural designs by referring to something outside architecture, that formal and visual qualities are of secondary importance in architecture, has not just accidentally happened to dominate contemporary thinking about architecture. It has its own history and originates in a number of philosophical and psychological positions that became influential in the 1960s. While these positions have in the meantime ceased to be credible in philosophy and psychology, they have remained enshrined as dogmas in the writings of architects, architectural theorists, and historians. (Arguably, the same problem exists in many other fields of the humanities.) In other words, much of contemporary architectural thinking is based on assumptions that have lost their credibility in the disciplines from which they were originally imported into architectural theory—such as the view that all thinking is verbal, that there is no innocent eye, that perception is inseparable from our beliefs, that everything is text. Nevertheless, these views have been preserved, as fossilized sacrosanct dogmas, in contemporary architectural thinking. They continue to serve as justification for the disregard of visual and formal considerations in architectural design. And they have had a remarkably negative impact on the visual qualities of our built environment: for a number of decades, generations of architects have been taught to ignore visual and formal issues in their designs and to concentrate on the meanings, stories, and symbolism that can be told about architectural works. It is consequently no wonder that our cities look the way they do.

The intention of this book is to help overcome the current situation. It is not meant to be a scholarly work. Rather, it has a mission to perform. It was written in order to undermine the positions that have hugely contributed to the formal pollution of our visual environment. If it is to achieve its purpose, the book should reach as wide a public of architects, architecture students, and academics as possible, and it should convey its message clearly. I have therefore made every effort to make it popular and I have yielded to scholarly impulses only in one detail: knowing that I am presenting material that has been little addressed in recent writings on architectural theory, it was necessary to footnote properly and direct interested readers to the current bibliography on this topic.

ACKNOWLEDGMENTS

My gratitude must first go to the painter Ivek Grabovac, who prepared me for the study of architecture when I was eighteen. Ivek taught me not only to draw but also to look and see shapes as such. The awareness of the autonomy of the visual-spatial realm that I received in his drawing classes decided much of my later intellectual development. After architecture I studied philosophy, and owing to my awareness of things visual I simply could not take seriously the linguistic turn and the idea that all thinking is verbal. Similarly, in the early 1990s, when I began my doctoral studies at Penn, I had to realize that deconstruction and phenomenology, the two dominant paradigms in then-contemporary architectural theory, were programmatically anti-visual and could not satisfy my theoretical concerns.

Since 2000, the old dogmas of the linguistic turn, cultural constructivism, and antirealism have lost their credibility as a result of psychological and philosophical research on human thinking and visuality. Many friends, colleagues, and students have contributed to this book by discussing these matters with me, as well as the content and organization of this book. I owe special gratitude to Mike Austin, Lars Blunck, Adrian von Buttlar, David Chaplin, Jovan Djerić, Peter McPherson, Cameron Moore, Kristof Nyíri, Tony van Raat, Predrag Šidjanin, Milan Šijakov, Radovan Štulić, Bojan Tepavčević, Dejan Todorović, Ian Verstegen, Richard Woodfield, and Nick Zangwill. Many of these people work at the University of Novi Sad, and I am grateful to Nadja Kurtović-Folić for having enabled my collaboration with that institution. Decisive advice about the formulation of the content and the selection of the illustrations came from Marc Bailly and Mark Gage; it is to them that I owe my awareness of the contemporary formalist trend among the younger generation of architects. Marc and Mark, together with Florencia Pita, Michael Hansmeyer, and Damon Brider have kindly allowed me to include the illustrations of their works in the book. As always, my home institution, Unitec Institute of Technology, provided help and support for the various phases of the project. My special gratitude to my proofreader, Karen Wise, for her help with written English and to Carley Lockie and Arnika Blount for the technical preparation of the drawings. Finally, book authors have their private lives, and mine has become much more enjoyable since, in the course of writing this book, I discovered the art of squash. I therefore owe much to Philip Schmidli, who has been teaching me the art, has become a very close friend, and has made my New Zealand isolation infinitely more cheerful.

VISUALITY FOR ARCHITECTS

1 Khaosiung Pop Center, Gage/Clemenceau Architects

INTRODUCTION

The final decades of the twentieth and the opening years of the twenty-first century brought about a revolution in the understanding of human visuality. The psychological doctrines about human perception and visual thinking that had remained undisputed for decades were discarded one after another, as a result of new discoveries and the theories that derived from them. A lack of awareness of these changes is a remarkable aspect of contemporary thinking about architecture, especially since they have occurred while, as a result of the introduction of digital media, the architectural profession and academia have been intensely revising their understanding of human visuality. The two philosophical paradigms that have dominated architectural theory in recent decades—deconstruction and phenomenology—insist in various forms on the primacy of language in human thinking.[1] They take words as the model of human interaction with the world. The implication is that these paradigms have a difficult and complex relationship to human visuality that often includes its explicit denial. The generations of architectural academics and theorists whose intellectual framework was formed on Derrida and Heidegger are unlikely to consider or read contemporary works on the psychology or philosophy of perception. At the same time, owing to breakthroughs in the philosophies of mind and perception, academic discussions about topics such as the meaning of architecture, authenticity, writing versus speech, and the absence of presence have become obsolete and antiquated. In addition, architects' attention has been redirected to new challenges that have resulted from the introduction of digital media in architecture. In this situation, contemporary research in the philosophy of perception and cognitive psychology provides important insights and the only credible framework for responding to new challenges.

This book presents a clear and easy-to-follow introduction to the contemporary understanding of human visuality. Strictly speaking, visual and formal are not the same—but, as we shall see, the contemporary theories of human visuality vindicate emphasis on form in architectural aesthetics. The book is written for architecture students, academics, historians, and theoretically minded practitioners. It aims to achieve an architecturally relevant articulation of current debates in the philosophy of perception and cognitive psychology. The form of these debates and the dramatic changes in the understanding of human visuality that have occurred in recent decades determine the organization of the material. One of the central themes of the book pertains to the contribution of conceptual knowledge to human visuality. For a very long time, the standard view has been that an individual's perception is always already predetermined by that person's thoughts, knowledge, ideas, and expectations. In other words, that perception is inseparable from classification or interpretation. In architectural and art history this view has been known as the thesis that there is no innocent eye. This position was popularized by Ernst Gombrich and is based on the psychological theories of the 1950s. Cognitive psychology has, however, made huge progress since those days. Gaetano Kanizsa's research on the phenomena of completion has provided important new insights in the understanding of the difference between seeing and thinking, while the groundbreaking research by David Marr and Zenon Pylyshyn has introduced a differentiation between *early vision*, which is impenetrable to our conceptual thinking, and the higher visual mental processes that perform object recognition.[2] "Early vision" is the stage in perception that provides us with the representation of the spatial layout.[3] In their survey of modern theories of human visuality, quite contrary to the positions that still dominate much of architectural theory and art history, Alva Noë and Evan Thompson state that the "orthodox view" in contemporary psychology assumes that "perception is thought-independent" whereby "the beliefs and expectations of the perceiver are thought to have no influence on the character of the subpersonal computations that constitute perception."[4] Unlike two decades ago, today it is possible to talk about purely visual and formal interaction with architectural works, independent of our concepts and ideas associated with them.

The implications of the concept of *early vision* for architectural theory are revolutionary: if our conceptual thinking cannot affect our perception and spatial thinking, and if the latter are essentially "hard-wired," then a substantial body of twentieth-century debate about architectural space and visual communication needs to be revised. It becomes impossible to argue, as it has been argued many times, that spatial thinking is merely a product of one's cultural environment. Visual means of architectural communication need to be understood in accordance with these new paradigms. This is particularly obvious in discussions of the status of perspective. For a large part of the twentieth century, debates on perspective concentrated on understanding its role as a tool of communication. Was perspective, as a tool of visual communication, a unique development, merely a characteristic of certain cultural traditions (the Renaissance, ancient Greece), or was it a manifestation of wider, universally human, cognitive principles? In the contemporary context, this debate loses much of its significance. It has been replaced with the debate about the role of perspective in human visual thinking, constancies in human perception, and the nature of human visual space.

Modern studies on spatial-geometrical thinking, visual imagination, and mental rotation pertain to the mental processes that are equivalent to CAD-type computer programs. Visual imagination is another example of a mental process that is independent of conceptual thinking. It also does not depend on the use of language. Modern experimental research on the human ability to imagine spatial objects from different sides (rotate them in visual imagination) started in the 1970s.[5] For reasons discussed later in this book, before the 1970s research on visual imagination was dismissed as unscientific. Mental rotation and the ability to imagine spatial objects from different sides are nowadays simulated by various 3-D modeling programs; some decades ago, European architecture schools used courses in descriptive geometry in order to develop this mental skill in future architects. What psychologists describe as mental rotation is the same kind of task that is performed by computers in modern architectural practice.

Changes in the understanding of human visuality cannot fail to affect our understanding of human aesthetic interaction with architecture. It is still far from clear whether there may exist features of the human brain that incline humans to prefer certain shapes (including architectural forms) over others. Nevertheless, it is possible to discuss the aesthetic positions on architecture that can be credibly sustained today in the context of the modern understanding of human visuality. For decades, the view that what we see is determined by what we know and expect to see, that there is no innocent eye, meant also that architecture could not be evaluated or appreciated purely visually, on the basis of its spatial properties, shapes, and colors. If all perception is affected by our knowledge and expectations, then visual aesthetic judgments have to be affected too; there can be no purely visual aesthetic judgments.

The fact that our perception is impenetrable to our conceptual thinking radically undermines the credibility of this assumption. The idea that architectural works can be interacted with purely on the basis of their form and their visual properties is credible again. This situation not only coincides with but also provides theoretical support for the works of the youngest generation of architects who have revived interest in the formal, spatial, and visual aspects of architecture as a result of the introduction of digital technologies. From its beginning, the introduction of digital technology into architectural practice has been accompanied by an increased interest in formal-aesthetic properties of architectural works—one should mention here, for instance, Greg Lynn's discussion of supple architectural forms during the 1990s. We shall see in the final chapter that an argument formulated by the American philosopher Fred Dretske in the context of the debate about nonconceptual thought-contents actually explains why the introduction of digital media in architecture had to result in a revival of formalist interests among architects. In this book I include illustrations of works by Mark Gage, Marc Bailly, Florencia Pita, and Michael Hansmeyer as examples of this trend.

This book thus describes the philosophical and psychological environment of a major shift of paradigms in architectural theory that will have to occur in the years to come if architectural thinking is going to be credible at all. Changes in our contemporary understanding of human visuality impose boundaries outside which no architectural theory can assert credible claims. The book does not discuss those theoretical positions in modern psychology, such as neuroaesthetics, that may also influence architectural theory in the future but do not pertain to human visuality.[6] When presenting contemporary psychological theories and their philosophical implications, I have tried to write as clearly as possible, while not sacrificing the accuracy of the account. Obviously, this book cannot claim to make contributions to the philosophy of mind or perception or related psychological theories. But to the best of my knowledge, the problems and debates presented in this book have not been articulated in the context of architectural theory so far. I also hope that the book will contribute to the wider awareness of these topics among the architecture- and the visual arts–interested public.

1

ARCHITECTURE: FORM OR STORY

Here is a situation well known from studio design reviews in architecture schools. A talented student presents her work. She has spent much time resolving spatial and visual issues, the composition of spaces and the façade, the vistas created as one moves through the building. The scheme is a thoughtful response to the brief. She is hoping that the critics' comments will enable her to learn more about spatial and visual composition and the various strategies that she could have employed to make her building look better. At the same time, she is mildly dissatisfied with her studio professor: for the past six weeks he's been shying away from helping her with the visual and spatial problems she has been so passionately engaged with. More precisely, he looked bored every time she tried to discuss what the building looked like and how its spatial and visual qualities could be improved. But now at least, in the review, she hopes to get a more engaged response to her visual and spatial interests from this group of critics. And yet, even during her presentation, she notices the same lack of interest on their faces.

A short silence follows her presentation. The guest critic, who feels obliged to say something, comes up with a question: "Well, what is your theoretical position? I mean, your architectural question?"—one of those formulations that guest critics use when they feel obliged to help the student. Yet, for the student, the question is unexpected: it does not pertain to visual issues, the kind of problem that motivated her work. A theoretical position ultimately consists of statements one believes to be true or false—it does not pertain to what the building looks like. Although well intended, the critic's question redirects discussion away from her *spatial* and *visual* interests. Noticing the student's perplexity (she's got excellent grades in her theory courses, but how can reading Derrida help you decide about the color of the façade, or the shape of the window), another critic tries to save the situation by providing guidance: "What is the meaning of your building? After all, all architecture is an art imbued in meaning. Tell us in what sense your building is indexical?" Again a question that is irrelevant to what she was trying to achieve! How could meanings, ideas associated with a building have anything to do with, for instance, the visual problems that result from aligning spaces? While she is pondering this, her own studio professor, whose boredom by this time has turned into irritation, comes up with another question of the same kind: "We are asking, what is the meta-narrative for your project?"[1]

It is hard to imagine that the review can take a good turn from this point on; the critics will sit and try to be polite for another couple of minutes, but that is all. Nevertheless, the review is bound to make a strong impression on the students watching it. What they learn is that the only thing that matters is the narrative they can tell about their building. Many of them have come to study architecture assuming that it is a visual art; they now learn that the decisive aspect of design is storytelling. In the theory class they have already been told that everything is a text. Seeing the main thrust of this review, some students will busily try to concoct a narrative that will get them through the review when their time comes. A minority may stick to their old beliefs and risk a bad grade. A couple of students are likely to grow cynical: aren't these critics merely trying to impress each other by asking questions that sound intellectual? The dean is watching from the back, some of them have noticed; isn't the part-time studio professor who asked the question about "meta-narrative" merely trying to make impression in order to get a permanent job in the school? Isn't all this intellectualization, after all, merely indication of the critics' intellectual insecurities? Psychologically perceptive students may well come to that conclusion.

In fact, one should avoid being unfair to the studio critics. Anti-visual biases in contemporary architectural culture have a long history. The critics' attitudes were formed during their education and reflect the theoretical positions that have been widespread in architectural thinking for the past twenty years. The same tendency to base design on stories that can be told about architectural works is common in contemporary architectural practice as well. Here it is strengthened by the fact that in order to get commissions, architects often have to explain in words their design decisions to their clients. Sometimes they (are expected to) invent stories about what the building represents. But should such stories be mere tools to get commissions, or should they (and can they) really drive architectural design? For instance, in the eighteenth century a famous French architect proposed designing the house of a sawmill owner in the shape of a saw blade and the house of a well-traveled person in the shape of a terrestrial globe. His equally famous colleague and compatriot argued that the walls of a law court should be shaped in the fashion of the tablets of constitutional law.[2] These historical examples certainly have their modern counterparts. Some years ago I was present at a lecture where a prominent New Zealand architect described how he had designed a building placed near water in the form of a fish. It is hard to resist the impression that facile symbolism of this kind mainly reflects the architect's opinion of his clients—that he regarded them as shallow enough to find such explanation appropriate. But if this impression is true, then it would follow that he thought the same of his colleagues to whom he delivered the lecture, which is hard to believe. At the same time, he was obviously an intelligent man, and it was equally hard to believe that he himself took such crude symbolism seriously. I left the lecture puzzled about his genuine beliefs and intentions. In any case, architects need to get commissions, and it is extremely hard to avoid banality when design is driven by storytelling.

One should also bear in mind that it is impossible for architects to base the full range of their decisions about spatial and visual properties of the buildings they design on the stories they can tell about these buildings. Simply, it is impossible to fabricate enough stories to explain and justify all the decisions that need to be made about shapes, proportions, colors, composition of spaces, openings, penetration of light, and so on. A genuine belief that narratives can drive design can only result in the neglect of many of these considerations. It cannot fail to result in disregard for the visual and spatial properties of our built environment. Arguably, this is indeed what is going on, as can be evidenced by the visual and spatial qualities of our cities. Architects may need to tell stories in order to sell their designs to their clients—but problems start when they convince themselves that such storytelling can indeed account for the totality of relevant design decisions. My point in this book is that in both academia and the profession, this belief derives from the theoretical positions imported from other disciplines. It was not spontaneously created by architectural academics and practitioners. Nevertheless, very few architectural academics are aware of the origin of the assumptions on which they base their teaching. Practitioners who have been inculcated with these assumptions during their education have hardly ever had their origin explained. Let us therefore start by considering, in this chapter, how our current situation came about.

SEEING AND SEEING AS

It is certainly reasonable to doubt that the suppression of visual concerns in architecture could be possible at all. How could the architectural profession or academia suppress visual issues, considering that architecture is a visual discipline—often considered to be one of the visual arts? True, architectural works do have some properties that can be described only verbally (you can only state in words the function or explain the symbolism of a building). Nevertheless, it is certainly the visual presence of architectural works that dominates our everyday lives. It is hard to believe that disregard for visual aspects of architectural works could seriously become a major trend in architectural education or the profession. Yet, it is true that reviews like the one described above are common in architectural schools. Discussions of the narratives associated with buildings, the symbolism and concepts they express (as opposed to the discussion of their shapes or colors), dominate both architectural education and the profession. In the English-speaking world at least, it is hard to find architecture schools where students hear lectures about, for instance, the visual problems involved in staircase design or the composition of spaces. (Early in the twentieth century it was common to publish textbooks for the courses that taught such topics to architecture students, but such publications are nonexistent today.) One may try to explain the situation by saying that it is hard to teach and judge architecture on the basis of something so elusive as visual preference. It may be suggested that in an era when everything is considered relative and uncertain, judging architectural works on the basis of the narratives, concepts, or meanings associated with them provides a certainty that purely visual judgments do not have. But this explanation hardly suffices. Why should one expect to evaluate narratives and concepts associated with architectural works with greater certainty than the works' visual qualities? Why would preference for a certain story about a building be less elusive than preference for its shape?

In fact, much bigger issues are at stake. Architecture does not live in isolation from its intellectual and cultural environment. If anti-visual biases are going to be credible among architects, architectural academics, or theorists, this can happen only if such views are based on and derive from assumptions that are credible in the society in which they live.

Consider, for instance, the assumptions that one must make when complaining about anti-visual biases in architectural education or practice. This complaint makes sense only if one believes that some properties of architectural works are visual (such as shape or color) while others are conceptual and better described in words (such as function or symbolism). If one is protesting about privileging one of these aspects, one must believe that they both should be given appropriate attention. Additionally, one must believe that visual properties are not reducible to conceptual ones. Otherwise, the complaint would be pointless. The complaint therefore implies an understanding of human perception that one could call here commonsensical: the view that we must first perceive things in order to recognize what they are. You can't know what you are looking at before you've looked at it; you must see a thing first in order to recognize what you are seeing. If this is so, then what we see is independent of how we (subsequently) classify it, or the words with which we name it.

During the twentieth century, this commonsensical understanding of human perception was challenged and dismissed on various grounds by psychologists, philosophers, and art historians. The alternative view, which came to dominate the understanding of human visuality, was that perception is inseparable from recognition, that it is impossible to see without classifying (conceptualizing) what you see, that all seeing is always "seeing as."[3] The philosopher Marx Wartofsky said once that, according to this latter view, it is wrong to think that "in order to hit you, I must be able to see you."[4] Rather, what happens is that "if I see you, it is because I want to hit you." In other words, classification must precede or at least coincide with perception. Applied to architecture, this means that there are no visual properties of architectural works that are not ultimately derived from the ideas we associate with these works. Visual perception of buildings is merely a result of the knowledge and beliefs we already have about them. It is this view that still lingers, often implicitly and unconsciously, in much of contemporary discussion or writing about architecture. It pervades architectural education and hovers over the output from intellectually minded architectural offices.

REJECTING THE VISUAL

Arguably, whenever a visual artist feels compelled to explain the merits of his or her work by telling a story about it or stating what it means, symbolizes, or represents, he or she assumes that purely visual properties are not enough to justify the work. In other words, that the work cannot stand on its own. Such explanations are motivated by the belief that one needs to describe the work additionally, to state in words the ideas that should be associated with the work. In what follows I will call such a view *conceptualism*. It is opposed to *formalism*, which assumes that works of art and architecture should be judged on the basis of their purely visual and formal properties, independently of the ideas, concepts, or beliefs we associate with these works or stories we can tell about them.

The domination of conceptualism in contemporary architectural thinking is not just an accident—it derives from important intellectual developments in other disciplines that have shaped the understanding of architecture for the past fifty years. The critics in the studio design review described above did not ask just *any* questions; their questions reflected the views that are common today about what is important in architecture. Such views have not just *happened* to be widespread. They are a result of a series of specific influences that have affected architecture in the second half of the twentieth century. Conceptualism is not dominant because it is the only way to think about architecture; it is dominant because it has historically emerged as the dominant view. In order to understand the current situation, it is important to look at the history of why architecture is predominantly judged conceptually nowadays.

Originally, the idea that perception is inseparable from conceptual thinking became popular among visual artists in the early twentieth century.[5] Before World War II, a number of German right-wing philosophers and art historians advocated it, and they often combined it with the view that every mental activity, including perception, is a result of one's membership in a group, such as a nation, race, or culture.[6] Some of them argued that members of specific groups can only perceive what is meaningful for those groups;[7] others that perception is ultimately ethnically determined and that, for instance, a Japanese and a European perceive differently.[8] Through the so-called phenomenological tradition in architectural theory, and the writings of such authors as Christian Norberg-Schulz, this kind of position subsequently exercised a huge influence on English-speaking architectural academia after the 1960s.

After World War II, such ideas ceased to be merely philosophical theories and became subject to experimental elaboration by American psychologists. In 1947, in a groundbreaking experiment, the psychologists Jerome Bruner and Cecile Goodman examined the ways in which the value that people attribute to physical objects affects their perception.[9] The psychologists' hypothesis was that the greater value one attributes to something, the bigger this thing will visually appear to that person. This may sound like a strange proposition, but Bruner and Goodman tested it by examining schoolchildren's perception of the size of American coins. The children were asked to adjust an iris-type opening on a mechanical device to the size of different American coins. In some versions of the experiment, the children were asked to do this by memory, while in others they were looking at the coin, placed six inches from the opening, while adjusting the iris. A separate group of children were asked to do the same thing but while looking at gray cardboard disks of the same sizes as the coins—this was the "control group." Children in this last group performed their task with very good accuracy. But the children who were asked to adjust the iris opening to the size of coins (whether by memory or by looking at the coins in front of them) substantially overestimated their size—in the case of the quarter by 35 percent on average. Even more interesting was the fact that the social background of the children affected their responses. Bruner and Goodman found out that children from less affluent backgrounds overestimated the size of coins by twice as much as those from affluent background. The implication is that perception is inseparable from concepts, knowledge, beliefs, and values associated with the object of perception. In the case of architectural works, this would mean that one cannot perceive (let alone contemplate) their shapes independently of the ideas and concepts that one associates with these works.

In another experiment, Bruner examined how people's expectations affect perception.[10] The experiment consisted of showing the subjects playing cards for very short periods of time (parts of a second). Some of the cards were the usual ones, such as five of hearts or seven of spades. Others were nonstandard, such as a black three of hearts, a red two of spades, and so on. It turned out that the recognition of nonstandard playing cards took much more time than the recognition of the standard ones. Some subjects completely failed to recognize that nonstandard cards were cards. Others reacted with perceptual denial: when shown a red six of spades, they would report "six of spades" or "six of hearts." The conclusion was that our perception is heavily influenced by our expectations.

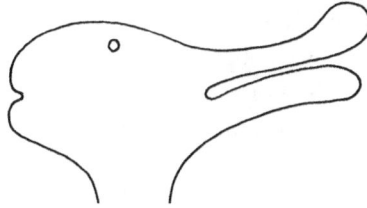

2 Duck-rabbit

In their time Bruner's experiments were a great success and triggered a virtual industry of similar research during the 1950s. Within a decade these studies started influencing philosophy, visual arts, and aesthetics. An argument that was often invoked in favor of the view that all perception depends on our previous knowledge involved drawings such as the duck-rabbit—the drawing can be seen as a drawing of a duck or a drawing of a rabbit, but never independently of our ability to classify it one way or another. A wave of psychological research concentrated on the ways in which our beliefs and expectations affect perception. This trend in the psychology of perception came to be known as "New Look" psychology. As the psychologist Ian Gordon observed twenty years later, the research literature of the 1950s

abounds in examples of perception being tricked in ways which reveal the involvement of knowledge, experience and familiarity. . . . Publications of the time describe oddly-shaped rooms which appear normal when viewed through peep-holes, pictures and figures which are difficult if not impossible to decipher without verbal hints, delays in recognizing briefly exposed words when these are threatening or taboo, and of course, many illusions. Showing the malleable and vulnerable aspects of perception under laboratory conditions increased the belief that this was how perception must be all the time.[11]

ARCHITECTURE AND ITS MEANING

By the early 1960s ideas deriving from New Look psychology started to infiltrate writings on art and architecture. A particularly widely read architectural articulation of the view that perception is inseparable from knowledge, beliefs, and previous experience was presented in Christian Norberg-Schulz's 1963 book *Intentions in Architecture*. Quite in line with New Look psychology, Norberg-Schulz argued that what happens in the eye or mind is irrelevant when it comes to explaining human perception. In his view, perception is merely the recognition of things already known—it fully depends on the concepts we operate with and results from the demands made by our society. "The given world consists of the objects we know."[12] Norberg-Schulz consequently rejected the idea that one can think about or perceive the shapes and forms of architectural works independently of the concepts associated with them. Immediate experience cannot be the point of departure for understanding architecture, he argued. In his view, "mass" or "space" cannot be taken for self-evident properties of architectural works. Rather, one can only perceive *meaningful forms*, since the perception of shapes is always accompanied by the awareness of their meaning. It is impossible to perceive things without meanings attached to them. Consequently, it follows that there can be no evaluation of architectural works purely on the basis of their forms: "That an independent, that is, meaningless form has quality, is an absurd statement."[13]

But when he had to present examples of such architectural "meanings," Norberg-Schulz was much less convincing. His examples tend to be arbitrary historical claims about architectural works of the past. He thus claimed that early Christian churches represented the heavenly Jerusalem; that the contemporaries of Gothic cathedrals conceived of them as heaven; or that during the Megalithic period symbolism was based on the cult of the ancestors.[14] In fact, none of these claims can be documented or historically proved, so they do not state the "meanings" of these architectural works but, rather, Norberg-Schulz's arbitrary guesses. Immensely influential in its time,

Norberg-Schulz's introduction of the latest scientific theories of human perception in architectural theory ultimately ended up as a justification of poor practices in historical scholarship. But the implications of the problem were by no means limited to historical scholarship. People do often agree about the aesthetic value of historical buildings, but if their "meanings" cannot be stated with any reasonable historical certainty, then it follows that "meanings" are irrelevant for aesthetic judgments.

"THERE IS NO INNOCENT EYE"

Outside architectural theory, Norberg-Schulz exercised little influence, and when it comes to the visual arts, Ernst Gombrich's discussion of New Look psychology was by far more influential. For many art historians, the publication of Gombrich's 1960 book *Art and Illusion* was the groundbreaking moment when the idea that perception is inseparable from classification and conceptualization entered their discipline. In the American context of the 1960s, one should not underestimate the influence of art historical academia on the education of architects. In those days doctoral programs in architecture were few, and future architectural academics often received their doctorates from art history departments.

The claim that "there is no innocent eye" is one of the central theses of Gombrich's book. By saying this, he meant that human perception is inseparable from classification.[15] Gombrich opposed the view that we first passively perceive and only then classify, recognize what we have perceived. In *Art and Illusion,* for instance, he wrote, "All thinking is sorting, classifying. All perceiving relates to expectations and therefore to comparisons."[16] In his view, nothing can be perceived without being simultaneously (or previously) classified as a certain kind of thing, or, as he stated, "To perceive is to categorize, or classify."[17] Gombrich's position was strongly influenced by the latest psychological research, but also by the views of his close friend, the philosopher Karl Popper. Popper dismissed the position that sense impressions are first received and only then conceptualized, that perception is passive reception, as "the bucket theory of the mind."[18]

Nevertheless, the view that all perception is based on classification is not unproblematic. One important problem, which subsequently troubled Gombrich for decades, goes as follows. Assume that I can perceive things only because I classify them in a certain way. It is then impossible to say that when perceiving, for example, a red and a blue ball, I first perceive the two balls as different because I perceive their individual colors and *then* classify one of them as blue and the other as red. Rather, I perceive the blue ball as blue and the red ball as red *because* I classify them that way. But consider then the question of *why* I classify things as red and blue. Either this classification is absolutely random or it is based on some properties of these objects (e.g., objects reflect light of certain frequency, which I perceive as color). If the classification of objects depended on the properties they possess, I would have to perceive these properties *before* and *independently of* classification. It has been assumed, however, that this is impossible, that there can be no perception independent of classification. But then it follows that our perception of things in the real world is *independent of* any properties of these things. We perceive properties of objects only because we classify objects as having these properties— and what we perceive has nothing to do with the real properties of things!

Gombrich vehemently opposed this view.[19] Nevertheless, he did state in *Art and Illusion* that "there is no reality without interpretation."[20] On the one hand, he fully subjugated human visuality to classificatory and conceptual thinking, while on the other, he was still trying to defend the view that, for instance, realist paintings represent objects by resembling them.[21] He still assumed that a painting can *objectively* resemble the things it depicts. Such a position appeared contradictory to many of his readers.[22] If all visuality is based on classifications, then it is ultimately a result of its social and historical context—after all, human beings learn to classify things from the specific social context in which they grow up. But then it follows that visual perception is as conventional as language or any other social institution. It follows that people perceive things as similar merely because they've been taught to perceive that way in the social context in which they grew up. Representation in the visual arts, it follows, can only be a social convention; different societies use different styles of visual communication *because they perceive differently.*

Gombrich's problems were aggravated by the fact that his book came out in the 1960s, a decade marked by the rise of the view that reality is constructed by the human cognitive apparatus, which, in its turn, is merely the product of an individual's membership in a group, such as culture. This is the view that our culture or language slices reality into things and properties. All our cognition, including perception, is conceived of as a result of this process. Reality is then merely a cultural construct that does not exist independently of our culturally derived worldview. In other words, it's not that there are real things in the world and they have properties. Rather, we are merely culturally conditioned to believe in the reality of the world and things with their properties. It is not that our culture influences our understanding of reality—rather, our culture *constructs* reality itself.[23] This view is sometimes called *antirealism.* The publication of *Art and Illusion* coincided with a number of other influential books that promoted various versions of antirealism. Consequently, to many readers, Gombrich's book appeared as the most important art historical contribution to the same wave of cultural relativism.[24]

TOWARD DECONSTRUCTION

Among architects, antirealist ideas became widespread with a substantial delay. They arrived only during the 1980s through the impact of deconstruction; ultimately, they were a result of French cultural influence. An important collateral implication was that they also arrived prepackaged with an additional emphasis on the importance of language for human thinking. In this case, the idea is not only that our cultural background slices reality and organizes our cognition but that this happens through language, because language is seen as inseparable from thinking. It should be mentioned that the idea that all thinking is verbal and always in a language is not a peculiarity of French intellectual traditions. It can be found in the works of the German early Romantic thinker Johann Gottfried Herder as well as later German philosophers, such as Martin Heidegger and Hans-Georg Gadamer.[25]

In any case, it was through its French articulations that the view that thinking is inseparable from language became widespread in the understanding of architecture in the 1980s and 1990s. Among the French, the idea was originally associated with the work of the early twentieth-century Swiss linguist Ferdinand de Saussure, who argued that words and concepts are comparable to two sides of the same piece of paper: you cannot cut one side of the paper without cutting the other. If this were so, there would be one-to-one correspondence between words and concepts (thoughts). Thinking would be inseparable from language.

Jacques Derrida, whose views came to dominate architectural thinking in the final decades of the twentieth century, added a new slant to Saussure's views. He assumed, following Saussure, that concepts and words categorize things in the world the same way and then observed that we use concepts in order to categorize things in the world. But then, since words are arbitrary social conventions (things are called what they are called because languages developed in a certain way through history), it follows that our categorization of objects in the world is merely an arbitrary linguistic affair. We think about (and perceive) things in the world as separate items with certain properties because the language we speak happens to classify them that way. This means that there is no reality beyond language, or as Derrida put it, there is nothing outside text.[26]

The influence of deconstruction in architecture therefore emphasized the significance of language as the paradigm for dealing with architectural works. Similarly, if one believes, as did Norberg-Schulz and other followers of Heideggerian phenomenology in architecture, that perception is inseparable from meaning, we finish again with a stance that replaces visual interaction with architectural works with narratives, stories, and ideas that are associated with these works. One commonly thinks that during the 1980s and 1990s—the period that decisively formed the current generation of architects and architectural educators—American architectural academia was marked by an intellectual confrontation between deconstruction and phenomenology. Because deconstruction was a defined architectural style, it may have seemed to dominate the production of the most famous architects at the time. But styles, like fashions, come and go. It is not at all inconceivable that phenomenological influences may have had a more profound long-term effect. Whatever the outcome, for our discussion here it is significant that neither of the two sides had much interest in the visual aspects of architecture: the debate was between understanding architecture as text or reconstructing meanings associated with architectural works. In both cases, the architect came to be considered as a public intellectual, someone who makes public statements through his or her works. Ultimately, both positions implied that it is the verbal, not the visual, that architects deal with.

In order to understand the position of the critics in the studio review described at the beginning of this chapter, it is important to bear in mind how the views that currently dominate architectural academia came about. The critics' questions were not just mere arbitrary intellectualizations. Rather, they reflect the theoretical paradigms dominant at the time when these critics received their education. Insofar as they may have been trying to impress each other, they were doing it using questions that, they could expect, would bring them recognition within the institutional framework in which they were operating. Their previous education taught them to relate to architecture through narratives. The fundamental assumptions in the environment in which they were educated were that there can be no perception without classification (conceptualization), and no classification without language—consequently, no consideration of architectural works without a narrative. The evaluation of architectural work is then reducible to the evaluation of the narrative associated with the work.

The only problem is that in the meantime philosophy and psychology of perception have progressed a long way from where they once were—today, they fully legitimize purely visual architectural interests. Architects and theorists have by this time spent decades meditating on Heidegger and Derrida, but meanwhile philosophers and psychologists of perception have moved on. As we shall see later in this book, modern theorists of perception would actually side with the student whose work the critics dismissed. Entrenched in the old dogmas that there is no innocent eye, that perception is inseparable from categorization, or that all thinking is tied to language, contemporary mainstream architectural theory is largely out of sync with the modern philosophy and psychology of perception. If architectural thinking is to overcome this gap, it needs to take into consideration the results of modern research in these fields.

2
THE EYE IS INNOCENT,
BUT THE BRAIN CAN BE A LIAR

The view that one cannot perceive a thing without recognizing it became influential as a result of psychological research on perception during the 1950s and 1960s. One of its implications is that architectural works cannot be perceived, let alone thought about, independently of the concepts and narratives associated with them. But whatever the architectural implications of this view, or its philosophical or psychological credibility, the view may appear fundamentally counterintuitive. It is reasonable to assume that in order to recognize what I am seeing, I must see it first. After all, light must first form an image on the back surface of my eye, the retina, if I am to see anything. Should the formation of that image not count as (the primary moment of) perception? At the same time, the image that light forms on the back surface of the eye is exclusively determined by the geometry of light rays. It is not affected by the fact that a person possesses or does not possess a certain idea, concept, or belief. If this is so, how could psychologists plausibly claim that perception depends on what we know or what we expect to see? This kind of reasoning often motivates those who try to think about architecture purely in terms of its visual and spatial properties. It is therefore important to understand first why this argument does not work. Only then we can discuss the possibility of purely visual and formal architectural interests.

VISUAL EXPERIENCE
The important point is that we do not actually see the image that light forms on the retina. Generally, a coherent representation of the world can be formed in our brain only if the information that our senses receive is combined and collated. This obviously applies to visual perception as well, since we have two eyes but we see one picture, not

two, of the world that surrounds us. The information that derives from the light stimulation of our two eyes needs to be fused into a single picture. This fusion has to be almost instantaneous: a creature that needed too much time to decide what was in front of it would have a poor chance of survival. Consider looking at a dinner table with five different objects on it: it certainly takes far less than a second to form a picture of these five different objects at five different depths. The fusion of each individual object must occur in much less than one-fifth of a second.[1]

In other words, the image that light forms on the retina is only a necessary stimulation of the human visual apparatus. It is a preliminary step in the process of perception, but not perception itself. The mental processes that convert the light stimulation of the back surface of the eye into visual experience are extensively studied by psychology, the cognitive sciences, and the philosophy of perception. The process starts when light enters the interior of the eye and the image of objects perceived is projected on the retina. When entering the eye, light passes through the eye's lens, and the image projected on the retina is actually inverted. But the image we see is not inverted—so this is a yet another example of the complex mental processing that constructs our visual experience. The retina contains light-sensitive cells which are not evenly distributed across its surface. The most sensitive area of the retina is near its center. It is called the yellow spot and is about four degrees in diameter. It contains the fovea, which about two degrees in diameter. The area of the retina where the optic nerve leaves the eye contains no receptor cells. This area is called the *blind spot.* (One can become aware of the blind spot by closing one eye and per-

3 Demonstration of the blind spot.

Hold the book one foot from the face. Close the right eye and fixate the drawing on the right with your left eye. Move the book toward your eyes until the left drawing disappears from your sight.

forming the simple demonstration described in fig. 3.) The blind area in our vision remains unnoticed as long as one uses both eyes because the blind areas of the two eyes do not overlap. Once again, the brain combines the information from both eyes into one image.

When we look with one eye, however, it is still not the case that we see nothing or just a black hole in the area of the blind spot. Rather, the brain fills in the missing parts to form our visual experience, even when no information from the other eye is available. This is an immensely interesting phenomenon: what happens is that the brain makes guesses on the basis of what is seen in the areas neighboring those of the blind spot.[2] The philosopher Daniel Dennett argued in the early 1990s that the brain does not perform much work in the process and that it merely works on the principle "more of the same."[3] In his view, the process is similar to knowing that the family dog is under the bed because its tail sticks out: one knows conceptually and can state in words that the dog is there, even though one does not actually see the dog. Subsequent experimental research by the psychologist Vilayanur Ramachandran has shown that Dennett was wrong.[4] When a picture of a bar (such as the one in fig. 4) is presented in such a way that the interruption of the bar coincides with the blind spot, the subjects see the bar as continuous.[5] Even if the two sides of the bar have different colors, the subjects still see the bar as complete, but they do not see the border where the two colors meet nor can they say where each of the colors starts.

To complicate matters even further, without us being aware of it, human eyes move in rapid movements called "saccades." Typically, a saccade occurs within one two-hundredth and one-twelfth of a second. The eye then pauses for a small part (say, a quarter) of a second and then performs another saccade. The eye is blind during the saccadic movement, and what we see, we see in the moments between these movements. While we often believe that our sight is glossing across an image or text, the eye never scans continuously. Rather, it performs a series of jumps (called "saccade fixations"). When reading, people will saccade to a single word, fixate it for a quarter of a second

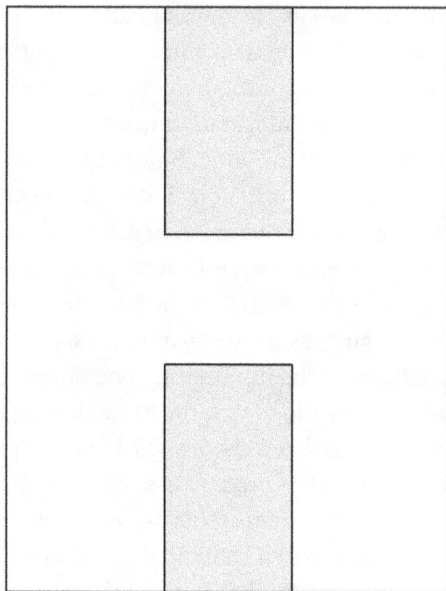

4 The interrupted bar is seen as continuous when this picture is presented so that the interruption falls on the blind spot.

or so, then reverse to an earlier word, then move further forward, and so on.[6] In picture viewing, too, the image we see is constituted from a series of disjointed snapshots that the brain has to put together into a coherent picture.

The processes that constitute our visual experience are therefore not to be reduced to the mere reception of light in the retina. Visual experience, the picture we actually see, is largely constituted by the brain, on the basis of the information it receives from the eyes. Once this fact is accepted, it is not hard to see how psychologists in the 1950s could come to the idea that what can be seen is predetermined by what the brain knows about.

BRAIN'S SIDE OF THE STORY: WORDS AND CONCEPTS
Although there are certainly no *physical* pictures in the brain, the image of things around us that we see is constituted by our brains. It

is not the same as the retinal image. But what is going on in the brain at the same time?

It was mentioned in the previous chapter that during the twentieth century both philosophers and psychologists were often inclined to think that all human thinking is verbal.[7] This position is likely to be highly counterintuitive to architects and visual artists: one often has to think and decide about the properties of visual objects (e.g., buildings) that have no names, such as color nuances and various shapes. These properties are often next to impossible to describe or think about in words. In many cases, decisions have to be made by imagining visually and drawing the building designed. Verbal descriptions are hardly of any use when making such decisions. Whatever the claims of philosophers or psychologists, if one insists that all thinking has to happen in a language, the attempts to describe, let alone explain, an architect's design process are bound to fail. We saw on the example of the imaginary studio review at the beginning of the previous chapter what happens if the architectural design process is reduced to its language-based components.

At the same time, those continental European philosophers who influenced architectural thinking the most (Heidegger, Derrida) during the final decades of the twentieth century argued for the primacy of language in human thinking. The same view was also shared by prominent mid-century English-speaking philosophers, such as W. V. O. Quine, Michael Dummett, Donald Davidson, and Gilbert Harman.[8] For decades, twentieth-century philosophy was dominated by the *linguistic turn*, the belief that languages are not only vehicles of communication but the actual vehicles of thought.[9] Among psychologists, during the middle decades of the last century the same view became influential as a result of the movement called behaviorism. Behaviorists tried to organize research in psychology according to what they regarded as scientific. They understood that science studies processes that can be measured, quantified, and described as material events. Since they did not know how to describe human thinking in terms of material and quantifiable material processes, they concluded that psychological research about human thinking must be unscientific and should be abandoned. In their view, psychology can only study human *behavior*. They consequently strove to convert the study of human thinking into the study of human verbal behavior. Some behaviorists even argued that human thinking does not happen in the brain but in the larynx—that thinking is the unpronounced movement of vocal cords. Behaviorists, as well as those philosophers who aligned with their views, such as Quine, insisted on the study of verbal behavior and denied the possibility of visual imagination. In an influential essay Quine explicitly claimed that it is impossible to visually imagine a building such as the Parthenon.[10] As we shall see in chapter 4, the decisive blow for behaviorist psychology came from the experiments of Roger Shepard and Jacqueline Metzler, who managed to show that quantifiable scientific research about human visual imagination was possible.

Until the 1990s, the philosophers who argued against the priority of language over thinking, such as Paul Grice, Jerry Fodor, and John Searle, were a tiny minority among their colleagues. Their important point, emphasized by Fodor, was that the sentences of natural languages often suffer from ambiguities and can mean more than one thing (e.g., "Visiting philosophers can be unpleasant"), while in his view, thoughts need to be free from ambiguities. If thoughts merely replicated the ambiguities of language, we would not be able to recognize when a sentence means more than one thing. The idea that all thinking is verbal is notorious for leading to very complex problems when one has to explain translation from one language to another.[11] The linguistic turn started to lose its credibility with the demise of behaviorism and the breakthroughs in psychological research on human visual imagination mentioned above. Visual imagination is obviously not a *verbal* thinking process. Another breakthrough in the rejection of behaviorism came in 1983 with John Searle's highly influential book *Intentionality*. Searle argued that the study of human thinking was not reducible to the study of human verbal behavior. Because of the important breakthroughs in the study of human mental processes that occurred in the 1990s, as well as research on the thinking of animals and pre-linguistic infants (children before they learn to talk), today the view that all thinking is verbal has become a minority view among philosophers and psychologists.[12]

The view that one could describe as standard among contemporary philosophers and psychologists is that people perceive, think, and then express their thoughts using words. This means that we have to differentiate between thoughts on the one hand and the words, phrases, and sentences that express them on the other. Some thoughts are true or false, and they are called *propositions*. Propositions are expressed using sentences. Other thoughts merely pertain to or identify something, without stating anything that could be true or false; such thoughts are commonly referred to as *concepts*.[13] Concepts are mental representations that list the classificatory criteria that something has to satisfy in order to be classified under that concept. (Philosophers sometimes call this understanding of concepts "the classical theory of concepts.")[14] A proposition then relates two concepts by saying that what is classified under one concept is also classified under another. The proposition expressed by the sentence "A cat is on the mat" states that something that can be classified as a cat can be also classified as something that is on the mat. Since people's thoughts are not language bound, it is possible to express one and the same thought in different languages: the concept that is expressed using the word "table" in English may be expressed using the word *tavola* in Italian.[15]

Among architects, the word "concept" can also mean many other things—for instance, any idea that triggered the design process or is vaguely associated with a specific design. Such "concepts" are often understood as spatial or visual, which is not the case with philosophical concepts. A "conceptual drawing" often refers to a drawing that expresses the idea of a building, but also a preliminary design sketch. In order to avoid confusion, in this book the word refers to the mental representations that specify the properties something must have in order to be identified in a certain way. If a person realizes that a thing satisfies the criteria of a certain concept, we can say that the person has *subsumed* the thing under a given concept: for instance, a person realizes that a certain thing is a chair. ("To realize" can often replace "to subsume under a concept.") A *definition* states the list of classifying criteria that something must satisfy in order to belong under a certain concept in a way that can be communicated (e.g., in a verbal form, by means of drawings, or in some other way).[16] One and the same concept can often be expressed using different words or phrases, in different languages, and can therefore have numerous definitions.

Arguably, our knowledge of a building's spatial properties is also a description and could be said to be a concept. The word "concept" can be also used for such mental descriptions. It is then conceived of as a concept whose content can be expressed in words only with difficulty. Its content is much better communicated using visual media, such as drawings. What then is the debate between a formalist and conceptualist about? The formalist can admit that a person who looks at a building from different sides or studies its plans can form a concept of the building's spatial properties. But he or she will insist that a genuine judgment of the building has to be based on the building's spatial and visual properties. It must not be related to other properties of the building we know about: whether it was designed by a famous architect, whether it was praised by a famous critic, what meaning the architect attached to it, what the general public believed, and so on. Obviously, conceptualists are those who insist on precisely such stories in making their judgments. A formalist may accept the use of the term "concept" for our knowledge of a building's spatial properties, but the important point is that the building should not be judged on the basis of other (nonspatial and nonvisual) concepts associated with it.

The debate about the nature of human vision, as described so far, can be summarized as follows: some theorists thought that vision was inseparable from conceptual thinking, and some theorists thought that conceptual thinking was inseparable from language—and some supported both views. In recent decades the view that thinking is inseparable from language has been largely abandoned by philosophers and psychologists, but it is still widespread in architectural academia. A dominant number of architectural academics today have received their education under the influence of theoretical and philosophical positions that advocated the primacy of language in human thinking. As a result, contemporary architectural theory often relies on assumptions that were abandoned in philosophy and psychology decades ago.

ANALOG, PROPOSITIONAL, DIGITAL

The debate about the nature of human vision and its relationship to conceptual thinking parallels the differentiation between analog and digital media. Since there is much confusion about which media count as digital or analog and why, it is important here to clarify this distinction.

In order to think and communicate about objects and shapes we need to represent them—in our minds, using texts, drawings, or on a computer screen. A drawing or a model can represent another thing because it resembles that thing: a blue surface in a painting represents blue sky because its color is similar to that of sky. An architectural model represents a building because of the similarity of its spatial properties to those of the building. Such representation is very different from the way a sentence describes blue sky or states that a building has three windows. The sentence "The sky is blue" does not resemble blue sky. We say that it describes (we may also say, represents) blue sky because it is a convention of the English language that words such as "blue" and "sky," when combined in a certain way, express a certain meaning. Representations by means of a language are *conventional*.

A representation by means of similarity, such as a drawing, is *continuous* in the sense that a part of a picture of a car represents a part of a car. The part of the drawing that represents a hood corresponds to the hood in real life; a part of the drawing of a hood stands for a part of a hood, and one could cut the drawing further and get representations of smaller parts of the car. But no part of the word "car" represents a hood. Rather, the word "car" consists of definite individual parts (i.e., letters) that are combined and, within the English language, this combination is a convention one uses to refer to cars.

Continuous representations, such as drawings, are called *analog* representations. Unlike words, they are typically nonconventional. This means that one does not need to know cultural conventions in order to identify blue sky with a blue patch in a drawing. Nevertheless, they can be conventional: old LP records used to record music by means of continuous representations (i.e., grooves) that would, when interpreted appropriately, be converted into a continuous line of tones. This conversion was performed by record players—they were the mechanical devices designed to apply a certain convention (e.g., the number of record rotations in a minute) in the interpretation of continuous grooves on an LP record. A modern CD disk, however, provides information in the form of consecutive electronic impulses, individual and separate quantitative units. A CD player will interpret these impulses as music. These impulses are not continuous; rather, they have individual numeric values. At the same time, they are so dense that when we listen to the tones that come out of the speaker, we hear the music as continuous. Such representation is *digital*. Similarly, an image generated by a digital camera looks like a picture and is indeed grasped as a continuous, analog representation. In fact, it records by listing the numerical values of individual, digital electronic impulses for each individual dot. The camera's reading device subsequently interprets the list of these digital values as color units. In this process, the device produces the picture that we see by applying certain technical conventions in interpreting these impulses. However, the representations of individual impulses are so dense that we do not see them individually. Rather, we see the total image that they make together. Ultimately, the resulting image that we get from a digital camera is comprehended as an analog representation: it represents blue sky using blue color. Such an image is an analog representation that is digitally generated by means of electronic impulses. The same applies to computer drawings, such as the images generated by CAD programs: what we see on the screen are analog representations generated by devices that process digital impulses.

The digital revolution in visual media has therefore not changed the analog nature of human visuality. Rather, it has introduced a new generation of digitally operating media in visual communication. Digital representations are always grasped in time: they are a series of impulses. Information conveyed in an analog form, however, can be given in a spatial (spatially looking) medium and can convey multiple pieces of information simultaneously.[17] Computer interfaces are a particularly good example. A computer itself is a device that operates by processing digital impulses. But this does not mean that human interaction with a computer is going to be particularly successful if it is based on digital principles. Old DOS-type operating systems that were used in computers in the early 1990s indeed included an interface that interacted with humans digitally. There were no icons and the computer screen presented only text—the lines of typed commands and the list of the actions the computer performed. All commands had to be typed and in order to do this, one had to learn them. Even operating a simple word-processing program required special training. Windows-based operating systems replaced this cumbersome interface with a picture of a field in which various icons can be selected. Rather than having to memorize dozens of commands, in modern word-processing programs one is simultaneously offered dozens of icons that one can perceive at the same time and choose from. A computer mouse communicates with the computer by means of digital impulses, but the job of a mouse is to enable *analog* communication: when one moves the mouse right, the arrow on the screen moves right as well. Because human interaction with the world is fundamentally based on visual experience and because visual experience itself is based on analog principles, Windows-style (i.e., analog) interfaces came to dominate human interaction with digital devices such as computers.

The parallel between computers and human brains is often ex-
ploited, and one may want to consider it here too. The image that
constitutes our visual experience is a product of our brain's activity. It
is constituted by collating signals that are received from millions of
brain cells—but we do not see these signals (the way we do not see
the electronic impulses that make up a digitally generated image). We
see the image itself, our visual experience. Ultimately, our conscious
visual experience of the world is analog, and as we have just seen,
digital technology has been developed precisely in order to deal with
this fact.

3
PERSPECTIVE AND ITS DISCONTENTS

Arguably, perspectival representations are *the* analog mode of visual representation. If it is accurate, a perspectival drawing will provide the eye with a bundle of light rays matching those that would reach it from the objects the drawing represents. Throughout the twentieth century, the validity of perspective as a method of visual representation was often denied by some art historians and philosophers. The resulting debates are often confusing. The literature on perspective is often partisan and tends to cite only the research that supports a particular view, even when that research is dated and was refuted decades ago. At the same time, psychological research on human vision provides new insights into the human understanding of perspective, visuality, and visual space. These insights require a revision of many twentieth-century misunderstandings that are still commonly found in the literature.

HOW PERSPECTIVE WORKS
There are few fields of human endeavor in which intellectual, artistic, and scientific problems are intertwined in such complex ways as is the case with perspective. Research on perspective requires a multidisciplinary competence that few people have. Debates about perspective may be very sophisticated in one discipline and yet make assumptions that are regarded as elementary errors in some other discipline. A number of times during the twentieth century theoretical positions on perspective were advanced, and became influential, while containing some very basic errors in reasoning. It is therefore useful to start by presenting a simple and straightforward explanation of how perspective works.

The easiest way to understand perspective is to imagine looking

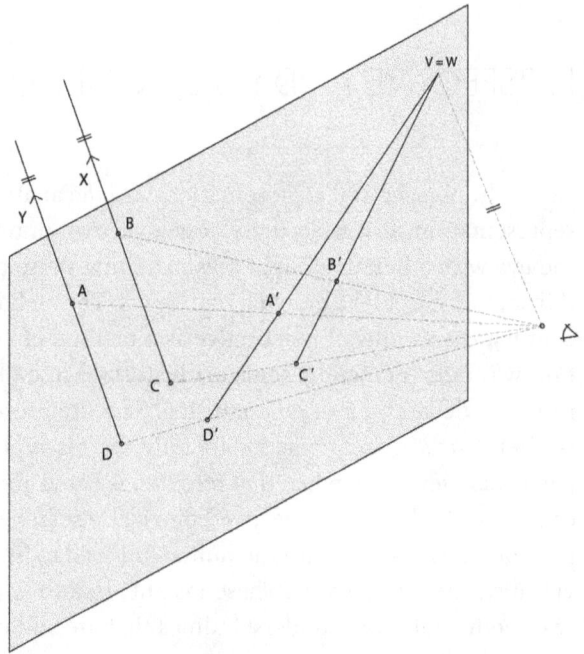

5 The picture of any line (e.g., AD or BC) behind the glass plane is the intersection of plane with the light rays that connect that line and the eye.

To understand the concept of the vanishing point, one should imagine that the given line (AD) is extended into infinity. Imagine then that a point (Y) travels to infinity along that line and that the eye follows its movement. As the point moves toward infinity, the line that connects it with the eye gradually becomes more and more parallel with the line along which the point is traveling. When the point reaches infinity, the eye will have to look in the direction parallel with the line the point traveled in order to see it. The picture of the point on the glass plane will be where the line that passes through the eye and is parallel with the given line cuts the glass plane (V). This is the vanishing point. There may be infinitely many parallel lines behind the glass (AD, BC, . . .), but since there can be only one line through the eye parallel with them, all parallel lines necessarily have one and the same vanishing point (V = W).

through a glass plane at a group of objects. Imagine drawing the contours of these objects on the glass. (The light rays that reach our eyes from the contours of objects are decisive for understanding the shape and spatial disposition of objects. Obviously, modern physics teaches that light is electromagnetic waves, but in our everyday visual experience light propagates along straight lines; things get occluded when another object is positioned between them and the eye. It is in this sense that one can talk about the geometry of light.) Now imagine trying to replicate this same drawing on a piece of paper. Perspective is a geometrical discipline that explains the geometrical procedure for accomplishing this; the principles of this procedure are explained in the caption to figure 5. A perspectival drawing made on a piece of paper is intended to deliver to the eye a bundle of light rays that match the light rays that define the shapes of objects seen through the glass. It will provide the same information about the shapes and dispositions of spatial objects that the drawing represents, and it will be read and grasped the same way.

A standard assumption when constructing a perspectival drawing is that the glass plane and the paper drawing are seen from the same distance and from the same angle and that they are flat planes. It is important to understand that this angle need not be orthogonal or that, ultimately, the drawing need not be on a flat plane or a plane at all. The plane may be curved, for instance. Historically, this has often been the case with fresco paintings on vaulted ceilings. One could therefore preferably talk about perspectival *representations*. A perspectival representation need not be a drawing, on either a flat or a curved plane. Rather, it may be understood as any disposition of objects and their properties that would deliver to the eye, when seen from at least one point in space, a disposition of light rays equivalent to that of the object (scene) it represents. (Under this radical reinterpretation, a physical model can be also understood as a kind of perspectival "representation"—but it is obviously not a drawing.)

A perspectival representation (or a drawing) is ultimately a matter of the geometry of light rays. It will be perceived and interpreted using the same visual and mental capacities that perceive and interpret spatial dispositions of objects. During the twentieth century there were a number of failed attempts to refute this view. Probably the most famous of these attempts was formulated by the art historian Erwin Panofsky in 1925.[1] Panofsky claimed that the capacity to comprehend perspectival drawings is merely a culturally acquired skill. He pointed out that the surface of the human retina is semi-spherical, while rules for the geometrical construction of perspective are normally defined for the flat surface of a drawing. Consequently, the geometrical rules that define the retinal image and those for the construction of flat perspectival drawings must be very different. It follows, Panofsky concluded, that a perspectival drawing cannot be representing things the way we see them. He further inferred that the capacity to comprehend perspectival drawings is a mental skill that Westerners developed at the beginning of the Renaissance. The implication is that this ability is a result of ingrained cultural habits. It has nothing to do with the physics or geometry of light rays. However, the problem with Panofsky's argument is that we do not see the retinal image. We see objects in space by receiving light from them. A perspectival drawing replicates the same disposition of light rays reaching the retina as the one that would be received from the objects the drawing represents. Panofsky was wrong because the shape of the retina is ultimately irrelevant.

A similar argument that is sometimes used against perspective pertains to the fact that we can comprehend the spatial dispositions of objects that perspectival drawings represent even when we look at them from different positions.[2] Yet, geometrical rules for the construction of perspectival drawings are always defined for the viewer in a certain position. The implication would be that our capacity to read perspectival drawings is independent of the geometry that defines these drawings, and that this geometry is merely a social convention. However, there is a geometrical explanation for our ability to comprehend perspectival drawings even if we are not looking at them from exactly the position that they are intended to be seen from. Let us ask what we see when we look at a perspectival drawing from a vantage point that the drawing was not made to be seen from. Simple geometry shows that in that case, depending on the angle, we see a deformed version of the original drawing. (See fig. 6.) In other words, assume that a drawing was intended to be seen from one position but we perceive it from another position. What do we see? The only way to answer this question geometrically is to draw another perspectival drawing that would demonstrate what is seen from the new vantage point. Again, one would imagine having placed a glass plane between the eye and the object—in this case the object being a perspectival

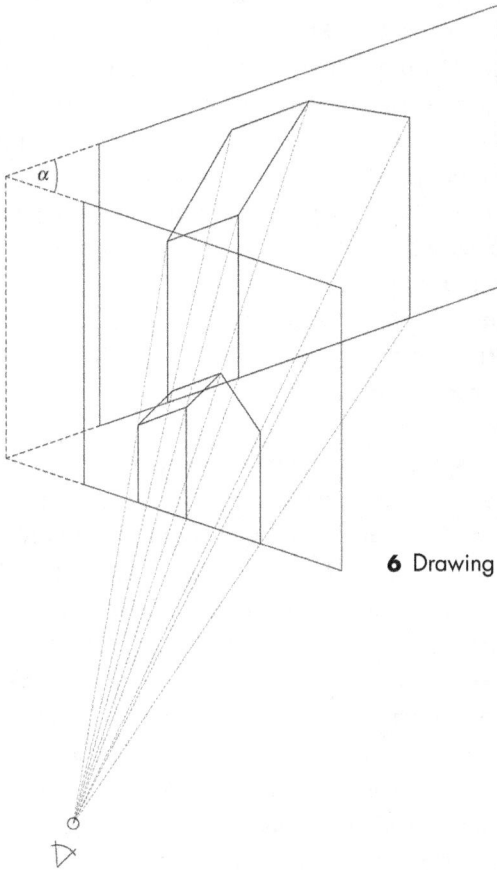

6 Drawing seen at an angle

drawing seen askew. This original perspectival drawing would now project another perspectival drawing on the glass plane. If the angle between the position the original drawing was intended to be seen from and the new drawing is small, the new drawing will differ little from the original drawing. But it can become unrecognizable as the angle increases.

PERSPECTIVE AND THE ANTIREALISM DEBATE

During the 1960s and 1970s, the status of perspectival representations became important in the debate about antirealism (discussed in chap. 1). The idea that perspectival representation is a social convention was strongly argued by proponents of the thesis that reality is merely a cultural construct—those authors who believed that membership in a culture organizes our experience into the reality that we perceive. A prominent promoter of such views was the Harvard philosopher Nelson Goodman. He was also a major critic of the view that perspective represents by delivering the same bundle of light rays as the disposition of objects represented. In his book *Languages of Art*, Goodman presented a series of "geometrical" arguments against perspective. With one exception (to be discussed in the next chapter), all these arguments were wrong and based on the miscomprehension of the concept of a picture plane.[3] But what mattered were the implications of his attack on perspective. The attack was meant to enable the claim that there can be no objective resemblance between an artwork and what it represents, that representation cannot be based on objective resemblance. In his view, all resemblance is a result of one's membership in a culture; people observe resemblances as a result of the culture they belong to. This would imply that no representation can be based on factual similarity with the thing represented. People merely perceive things as similar because they belong to certain cultures, but there is no *objective* similarity. By making this claim, Goodman targeted the concept of realism in art. In his view, one cannot argue that a picture is more realistic because it provides a greater amount of information about the object it depicts. Rather, "the touchstone of realism" lies not in the quantity of information but in how easily it issues, how stereotyped the mode of representation is.[4] Goodman inferred that any similarity between a painting and what it depicts is always relative to a given culture or person at a given time. In his view, there is no such a thing as objective imitation in the visual arts; there is only cultural inculcation of certain ways of seeing things.[5] The fact that we perceive similarity between things and their depictions is then merely a result of culturally ingrained habits. It is not that things really have some properties (that sky is blue) and paintings represent these things by having the same properties (a blue patch representing sky). Rather, we are culturally conditioned to see that there is sky, that it is blue, and that the same color is in the drawing.

As noted above, in spite of his attempts, Goodman never managed to show that perspectival drawings do not represent by delivering the same bundle of light as the objects they represent—and without proving this, his entire theory, although it was once influential, is merely a collection of arbitrary claims. But one should mention here an interesting experiment concerning the role of culture in the acquisition of the ability to comprehend images that was conducted in the early 1960s by the psychologists Julian Hochberg and Virginia Brooks.[6] They raised their child without any exposure to pictures. They took great care to remove any pictures from the child's vicinity. They even removed labels from cans and bottles. The child was never exposed to the idea of a relationship between words and pictures, never told that pictures represented anything. They never even read a story from an illustrated book to the child. But just before the age of two, when he had a reasonably large vocabulary, the child was presented with pictures of various things and asked what they were; he labeled almost all of them correctly. Human visuality, we can conclude, is more than a result of cultural inculcation.

During the 1960s anthropologists made a number of attempts to establish whether the ability to comprehend perspectival representations, photographs, and pictorial representations in general is a universally human or a culturally acquired ability. Some anthropologists reported that individuals belonging to cultures that had had little or no prior exposure to pictures had difficulty in identifying familiar objects in pictures.[7] Subsequently, these studies were criticized for the use of ambiguous tests or unclear task directions given to the subjects. In 1977 Jean Dirks and Eleanor Gibson tested the ability of five-month-old infants to recognize pictures of familiar faces.[8] Their experiments relied on the principle of (dis)habituation—the fact that children lose interest in things they have already seen and consequently look for a shorter time at them when they (re)appear. In Dirks and Gibson's experiments, infants were first shown a live smiling face a number of times. After that, a life-sized colored photographic slide of that same person or of a novel person was shown in the spot where the live face had previously been shown. The result was that when a live face was followed by the photograph of the same person, looking time decreased, while it increased if the photograph showed an unknown person. The conclusion was that five-month-old infants can perceive and recognize the face in a photograph. The capacity to comprehend pictorial or photographic representations, in that case, cannot be culturally acquired.

CONSTANCIES

The fact that perspectival drawings replicate the bundles of light that would reach our eyes from the spatial dispositions of objects they represent does not mean that our *visual experience* itself, the visual representation of things we see, is organized according to the principles of perspective. We have seen in the second chapter that there is a long way from the stimulation of the retina to the pictorial representation we see. The brain actively interferes in some phases of the process that generate the image we see. The retinal image itself results from optical laws, but this is not necessarily the case with visual experience. The latter is generated by the brain. It is therefore important to ask whether our visual experience itself is organized according to the laws of perspective. There exists a substantial body of psychological research suggesting that the spatial organization of human visual *experience* (the image generated by the brain, that which we believe we perceive) in some aspects significantly departs from the principles of perspective—and that it is also very similar in some other aspects.

Since the early decades of the twentieth century, psychologists have made huge efforts in the study of the phenomenon called *constancies*. Constancies in our vision occur when an object's shape or size is accurately perceived although, according to the laws of optics and perspective, it should not be. These are the situations, for instance, when the apparent size of an object may scarcely change although its distance changes significantly, or when the real shape of an object is perceived although the object is seen at a slant. The term "constancy" is used because size or shape is perceived as constant, independent of the distance of the object or its slant—the situation when the visual angle changes but shape or size remains constant.[9] In psychological terminology, one differentiates between the *distal* and *proximal* stimulus. Distal stimulus is the very object perceived, the proximal stimulus its image on the retina, generated according to the laws of optics and perspective. The retinal image is determined by the geometry of light rays, and it strictly replicates the size of the visual angle between the light rays that reach our eyes. If one and the same object changes its distance from the eye, the farther it is, the smaller angle of the visual field it will take—and the retinal image (i.e., the proximal stimulus) will decrease in size. Similarly, if we look at a circle at a slant, then its retinal image will have the longest and the shortest diameter. The proximal stimulus in that case should be an ellipse and not a circle. However, this is not what most people see. Human visual experience, psychologists often point out, tends to follow the *distal* stimulus. The proximal projection of an object (i.e., its projection on the retina) can have different shapes if the object changes its slant. However, psychologists say that for most people "the object appears to retain its shape,"[10] and the "perceived shape usually corresponds to objective shape."[11] Consequently, shape (or size) constancy is the phenomenon in which the percept of the shape of a given object remains constant despite changes in the shape of the object's retinal image.[12] The idea is that "we see them [objects] not in the shapes indicated by the laws of perspective but in the shapes which these figures 'really' possess."[13]

The implications of such an understanding of human visuality are likely to disturb many architects and visual artists. Psychologists actually mean that, for most people, when the angle of the visual field that the object takes (i.e., its visual image on the retina) shrinks with distance, the object is still nevertheless perceived the same.[14] For instance, if we look at two chairs of the same shape and size, one of which is at a distance of six yards and another at twelve, they will be perceived as being of equal size.[15] Another similar example that is often mentioned in the psychological literature pertains to the perception of the size of an approaching person.[16] According to geometrical optics, a person's visual height must double as he or she approaches the observer. Most people, psychologists say, will report that, nevertheless, the perceived size of the person has remained the same. Such examples obviously contradict the principle that things that are farther away are perceived as smaller. Another example psychologists often cite pertains to the shape of plates on a table seen from the side. They say that "when we look obliquely at a circular object, we see it not as an ellipse but as a true circle."[17] As a result, seen from the side a plate looks what it "really" is, circular, not elliptical as its retinal image would suggest.[18]

For many architects and visual artists this kind of view is likely to be very controversial. Many of us instinctively believe that when we perceive circular plates at a slant we see them as elliptical; certainly, chairs or people who are farther away are perceived as smaller than those closer to us. It seems fair to say that we perceive slated circles as ellipses, but that we know that they are circles—that we do not *perceive* circles. (This view, psychologists describe, is often stated by psychology freshmen.)[19] It is enough to hold one's hand next to the line of sight of a chair across the room in order to see that the image of the chair appears to be smaller than that of the hand.[20] Nevertheless, psychologists often insist on distal vision, and their tests seem to suggest that most people are used to seeing distally and not according to the laws of perspective.

CONSTANCIES DEBATE

In order to understand the problem better, one should consider briefly the history of the debate about constancies. It goes back to the Gestalt approach to psychological research that became influential in the years before World War II. Gestalt psychologists emphasized research on constancies in order to attack a methodological position they called *introspectionism*. Introspectionism was the view that one should differentiate between pure sensation and perception (the latter understood to include knowledge). According to introspectionism, sensation is to be strictly differentiated from the conceptual contents associated with its content. What we see should not be assumed to affect the study of how we see. According to this view, it is not correct to say that one sees a book or a desk: what one sees are bundles of light reflected by some objects, but in order to say that one sees a book or a desk, one also needs to recognize the object as a book or a desk.[21] The use of words such as "book" or "desk" relies on our knowledge about a specific class of objects to which the individual object belongs. Pure seeing, the argument goes, should be independent of such knowledge. When discussing human sensations psychologists should separate such acquired meanings from what is seen. Introspectionism assumed that what is seen consists of simple sensations. One of the founders of Gestalt psychology, Wolfgang Köhler, opposed this view, writing that "objects exist for us only when sensory experience has become thoroughly imbued with meaning."[22] Consequently, Gestalt psychology became attractive for those architectural and art historians (such as Norberg-Schulz or Gombrich) who wanted to claim that there is no innocent eye.[23] From the introspectionist point of view, people associate ideas with objects they perceive as a result of their previous experience and personal biography. These meanings associated with what is perceived can only derive from individuals' previous accidental experiences. If we were to assume that they affect what people see, we could never say that two persons see the same thing the same way. Introspectionists assumed that sensation was independent of an observer's knowledge, beliefs, or changes in his or her attitudes. Köhler criticized this view on methodological grounds. According to his criticism, introspectionism excluded experimental results that did not conform to the theory that these experiments were actually intended to prove.[24] Gestalt psychologists like himself aimed to redirect psychological research to the immediate spontaneous perception of everyday experience. Consequently, they insisted on the study of constancies.

Attempts to establish experimentally whether human vision is indeed organized according to the principle of constancies have a long history. As early as 1931 the British psychologist Robert Thouless presented tilted circles to his subjects and asked them what they saw—a circle or one of the ellipses from a given catalog.[25] The subjects reported that they saw ellipses, but these ellipses were closer to a circle than the ellipses they should have seen according to the laws of perspective. Their perception was a compromise between the real shape of the object and what the laws of perspective predicted. It indicated a "tendency to constancy," as Thouless put it, but the subjects did not perceive constancies properly. Psychologists further explored what happens if the subjects do not know what they are seeing—a circle or an ellipse. Cues that enable the subjects to establish distance or slant can be gradually reduced, but what happens then? In 1941 two other psychologists, Alfred Holway and Edwin Boring, found out that in such situations subjects' perception follows the laws of perspective—that is, people see slanted circles as ellipses.[26] Psychologists later established that perception also follows perspectival laws if objects (e.g., slanted circles) are illuminated for a very short time, such as one tenth of a second.[27] Constancy requires exposures longer than half a second.[28] By the late 1950s psychologists became aware that the responses they got from their subjects depended significantly on the instructions the subjects were given—that is, subjects could actually choose to take a distal or proximal attitude depending on how they understood what they had been told to do.[29] In other words, people can decide to make their perception follow either perspectival laws or the real shapes and sizes of objects.

Modern psychology therefore differentiates between objective and retinal perception. In a recent book that surveys the modern understanding of human visuality, Maurice Hershenson distinguishes between perceptual attitudes directed toward "object or linear size" and "extensivity or visual angle size."[30] (In the latter case, perception would follow the laws of perspective.) He reports that visual angle size, or the proportion of the visual field that the object subtends, is only brought into awareness with effort.[31] Similarly, the psychologists Irvin Rock and William McDermot state that although we do not see our retinal image, we see in terms of it.[32] In their view, Gestaltists have gone too far when emphasizing constancies: "The specific nature of the local proximal stimulus is available in some form to consciousness and [it is] not swallowed up, so to speak, by the more complex interactional processes of which it is only one part."[33] The modern understanding is that human visuality is therefore dual: most people can perceive in terms of objective sizes and shapes *or* in terms of visual angle. It is recognized that, in the case of most people, this latter attitude only needs to be brought to attention, but it is reasonable to assume that those of us who work in the visual arts and use perspectival projections in daily work will be used to seeing perspectively. Psychologists often state that attention to retinal (proximal) perception (i.e., the perception of the visual angle, which follows perspectival laws) is typical of visual artists.[34] Commenting on the implications of research on constancies for the visual arts, Gombrich noted that visual artists train themselves to see the world without constancies, to "break constancies" as he says, in order to be able to produce perceptively accurate drawings that will be appropriately interpreted, *with constancies restored,* by people who look at them.[35] He also pointed out that a visual experience that includes constancies violates visual occlusion of objects as defined by the geometry of light.[36] According to the laws of perspective, if I perceive a person standing in a doorway at some distance and then that person approaches me, as the perceived size of the person grows in my visual experience, it is likely to occlude the door. Simply, the visual angle of the person becomes bigger than that of the door, and the door is behind the person. But this will not happen if constancies are perceived: since the person is always seen to be the same size, the door will not be perceived from the beginning.

In a 2002 article, the psychologist Dejan Todorović summarizes the theoretical framework of the full century-long debate about constancies. Todorović differentiates between the distal, proximal, and phenomenal domain of human visual perception.[37] He sums up the current standard views in psychology by saying that perceived size can be understood as the impression of the *distal* size of environmental objects (the size as determined by a tape measure) *and* the conscious impression of pure *visual extent,* which is the amount of visual field covered by an object. In his view, this latter way of seeing is rarely used in the everyday life of most people—although it is according to this second sense that one says that "distant objects appear smaller." The proximal (perspectival) sense can be readily noticed and attended to, once it is pointed out, although, Todorović suggests, it is the distal sense that is almost exclusively used in everyday life by most people.

At the same time, it is in the proximal visual experience, when perceiving the visual angle, that our perception follows the laws of perspective. If we draw on a piece of a glass what is seen through it, visual experience documented this way will be organized in a way that corresponds to proximal vision. Many architects and visual artists, it is reasonable to assume, are inclined to see proximally. They are so used to doing it that they may not be perceiving constancies at all. (This is the case with the author of this book.) They may forget or not be aware that the general public, when seeing their works, sees them quite differently than they do.

4
PERCEIVING AND THINKING ABOUT SPACE

Perspective represents things, objects in space. Many architects will say, however, that they are not concerned with the design of buildings as objects—they are interested in buildings as tools to make spaces. From this point of view, it is spaces that architects design. After all, no person can live in the physical building, since the physical building is walls, bricks, concrete. Rather, people inhabit the spaces that are formed by these physical elements. An architect must then be able to concentrate, not on the physical elements of structure, but on the spaces these elements form. Thinking about spaces in architectural design is a bit like the perceptual difference between figure-ground.

The use of bearing walls in premodernist architectural traditions often resulted in paying great attention to the design of spaces. A good collection of such plans can be found, for instance, in the eighteenth-century map of the Roman Campo Marzio by Giovanni Battista Piranesi; figure 7 shows some of these plans extracted from the map. The approach does not necessary require symmetrical plans, as can be seen in the works of the American architects McKim, Mead, and White (fig. 8). This conception of architectural design, based on systematic forming, composing, and connecting clearly defined spaces that are conceived of as units, lost its appeal with the modernist introduction of "open plans." The open plans that one finds in Le Corbusier's works, such as those presented in figure 9, suggest an approach to design in which the physical building is designed, whereas spaces are a result of the disposition of walls. But in this case too, humans interact with these spaces—and since we mostly don't use plans when navigating buildings in our daily life, an important question for the architect is how to communicate the spatial organization of the building to the people that use it. The sixteen-century villa Rocca Pisani, by Vincenzo Scamozzi, is a particularly careful study of the

7 Selected building plans (*above*) from Giovanni Battista Piranesi's map of Campo Marzio

8 Selected plans of residential buildings (*right*) by McKim, Mead, and White

9 Selected plans of buildings (*opposite page*) by Le Corbusier

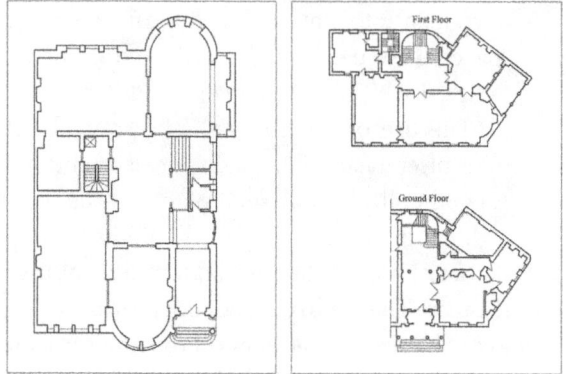

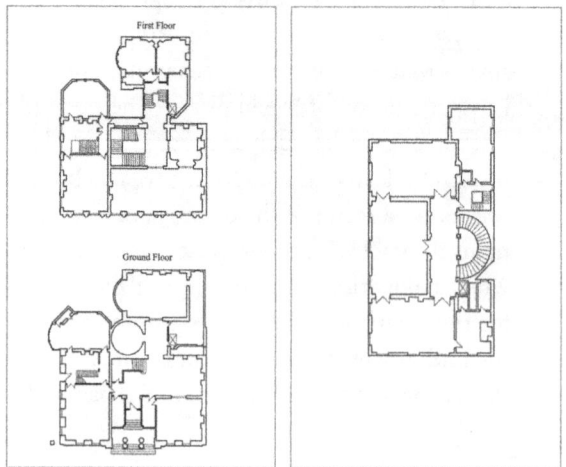

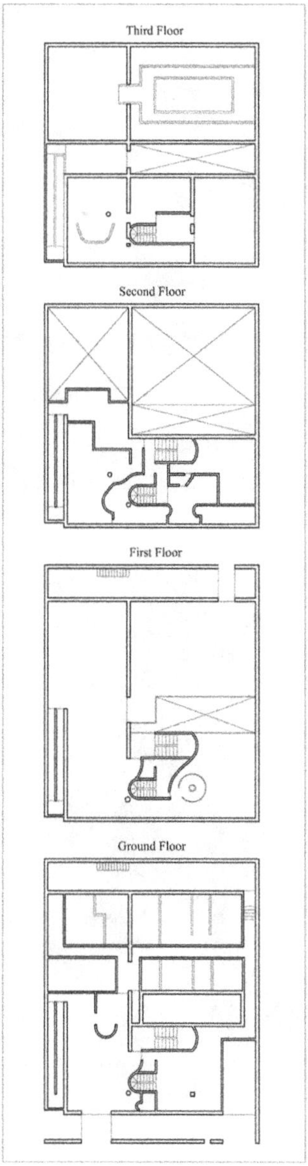

53

Third Floor

Second Floor

First Floor

Ground Floor

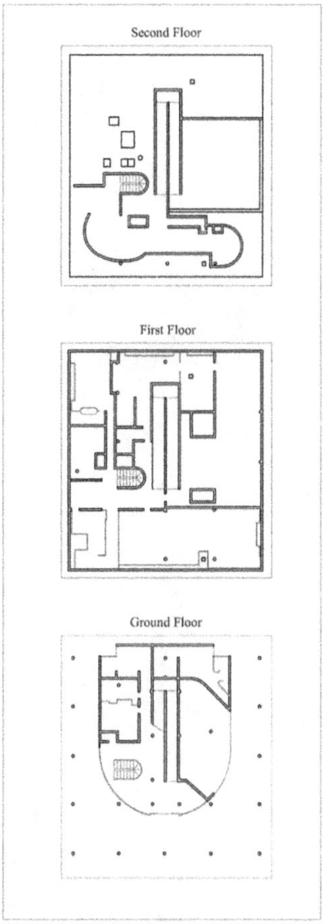

Second Floor

First Floor

Ground Floor

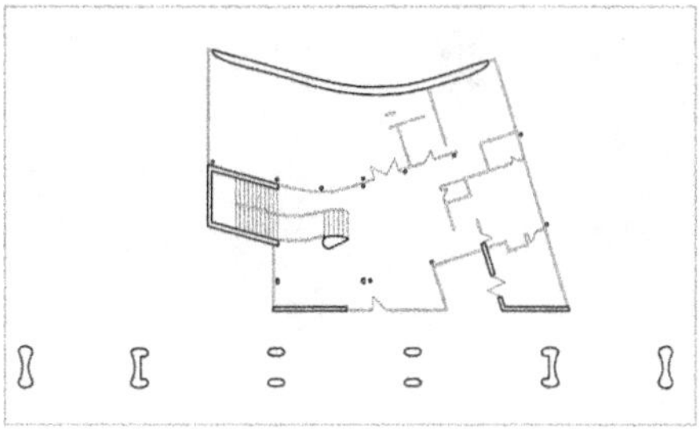

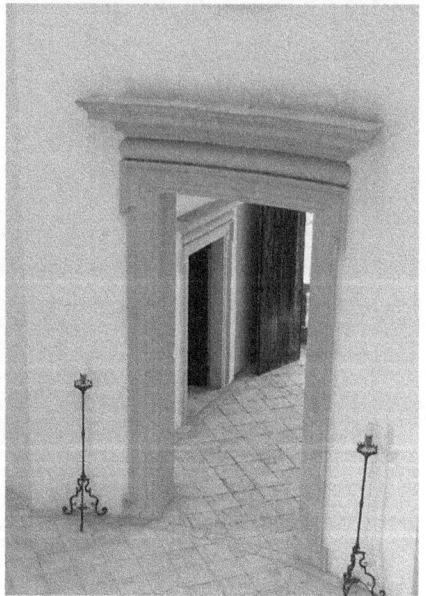

10–13 Villa Rocca Pisani
(*above and opposite page*),
Vincenzo Scamozzi

ways in which a building can communicate its internal disposition of spaces to a visitor. (See figs. 10–13.) The architect aligned openings in various directions so that one easily perceives the presence of spaces as one moves through the building. The columns of the portico are placed so that one perceives a tiny part of them as one looks from the central internal space through the main door: this clearly tells that behind the main door there is one more space, that of the portico. Such dynamic organization of spatial experiences often relies on opening vistas as one moves through the building. A good example is Damon Brider's project for the Cathedral of Auckland, New Zealand. (See fig. 14.) Except on important dates, such churches are often accessed through the side doors. In Brider's project, this leads to corridors that

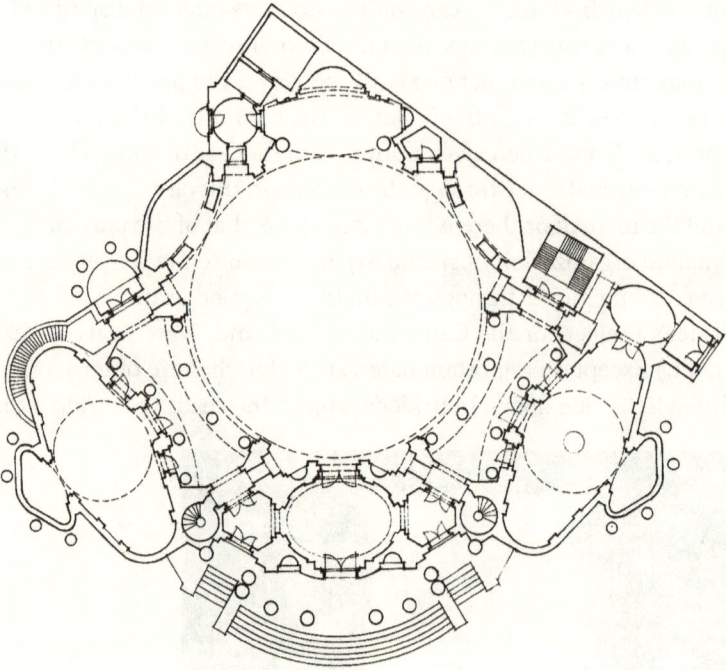

14 Project for Auckland Cathedral, Damon Brider

open to side chapels on one side and provide a vista of the lateral altar in the main space. Only as one enters the main space does one get the view of the main altar.

An architect's work is thus about designing spaces and buildings in space. But what kind of mental capacities enable us to think spatially and imagine buildings before their drawings are committed to paper?

SPATIAL PERCEPTION

The foundations of the modern understanding of the relationship between visual perception and the comprehension of spatial relationships were laid in the early 1980s by David Marr.[1] Before that, through the 1960s and 1970s, the *ambiguity of perspectival repre-*

sentation presented a significant problem for the understanding of human visuality. The important dilemma goes like this. Our experience of things in space is three-dimensional; we see things as three-dimensional objects. But this three-dimensionality has to be reconstructed by the brain from the two-dimensional retinal image. Like a perspectival drawing, the retinal image is defined by the geometry of light. The standard problem with perspectival representations of three-dimensional objects and layouts, however, is that they are *ambiguous*. This means that a single perspectival image can always be interpreted as a picture of infinitely many different three-dimensional shapes in space. For instance, a line in a perspectival representation may stand for a single line in three-dimensional space; but it may also be a representation of a number of disconnected lines that are merely perceived as a single line (appear to be a single line) from a specific viewpoint. (See fig. 15.) This applies to every line we see in space.

In the 1940s and 1950s, Adelbert Ames conducted a series of experiments examining the ways the human brain constitutes awareness of the three-dimensional properties of things on the basis of visual perception.[2] In one experiment the subjects were shown a crisscross of disconnected wires in a room; they were able to observe these wires through a peephole in the wall. The wires were positioned

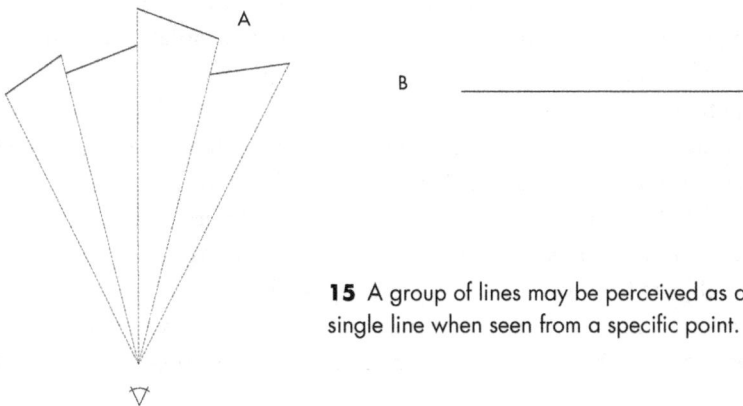

15 A group of lines may be perceived as a single line when seen from a specific point.

so that, although disconnected, their endpoints perspectively coincided when seen through the peephole. Observed through the peephole they were perspectively positioned to look like a chair. Indeed,
people looking through the peephole saw a chair, although in the
room there was merely a crisscross of disconnected wires. In other
words, when one perceives a perspectival picture, that same image
may have been generated by an infinite number of different spatial
dispositions of objects. Yet, our mind chooses one possible interpretation as the right one.

This ambiguity of perspectival representations played an important role in the debates about perspective during the 1960s and 1970s.
For Nelson Goodman (whose view that perspective is a social convention was described above), the ambiguity of perspectival representations was an important argument in his effort to deny the validity of
perspective as anything more than a cultural convention.[3] Goodman's
argument was as follows. Any perspectival drawing can be a representation of an infinite number of different dispositions of objects in
space. Nevertheless, our mind chooses to interpret it as a representation of one of them. Consequently, we must be culturally conditioned
to select this one single disposition of objects in space as the correct
interpretation. At the same time Ernst Gombrich, who defended the
transcultural validity of perspective against Goodman, regarded the
ambiguity of perspectival representations as a confirmation of his
thesis that perception is inseparable from conceptualization. In his
view, people looking through the peephole in Ames's experiment saw
a chair because their brain organized their perception according to
the available concept (chair). The availability of the concept explained
their interpretation of the disposition of wires they perceived.[4]

Modern psychology, however, provides a different explanation of
the way we derive our awareness of three-dimensional dispositions
of objects from two-dimensional images (the retinal image or a perspectival drawing). Explanations such as Goodman's or Gombrich's
will not work, because one can form a definite three-dimensional

interpretation of a two-dimensional image even when it is impossible to associate what one sees with anything we know or have seen in the past. As we shall see in the next chapter, it is possible to *individuate* three-dimensional objects without *identifying* them. Rather than relying on available concepts, our brain relies on specific rules or constraints when interpreting a two-dimensional image three-dimensionally.[5] For instance, a brain always interprets a straight line in an image as a three-dimensional straight line (although it may actually consist of a number of disconnected lines that only appear to be in continuation of each other). If the tips of two lines coincide in an image, they are interpreted as coinciding three-dimensionally. (This is why people perceived Ames's disconnected wires as connected.) Similarly, elements near each other in an image are interpreted as nearby three-dimensionally. Such rules and constraints determine the interpretation of our retinal image and provide us with knowledge about the spatial disposition of objects around us.

. . . AND THE PERCEPTION OF SPACE

The existence of these interpretative rules that define and enable our experience of three-dimensional space means that our comprehension of spatial relationships is not based on our previously acquired knowledge about things we observe. Rather, our capacity to interpret two-dimensional perspectival representations three-dimensionally seems to be hardwired. David Marr's work of the early 1980s provided a comprehensive account of the systems that must be in place if the human brain is to be able to interpret the retinal image as a representation of a spatial disposition of objects. According to Marr, the crucial moment in the process is the formulation of what he called a "2½D sketch."[6] This representation makes explicit the orientation and rough depth of visible surfaces. It defines contours and discontinuities in relation to the viewer. Subsequently, the brain forms the three-dimensional mental model that represents (describes) shapes and their spatial organization. The three-dimensional mental model is not related to the person perceiving the object. In other words, one first becomes aware of the spatial disposition of shapes and surfaces as perceived in relation to oneself, and then of their full three-dimensionality.

Should one assume that our perception is organized according to those geometrical principles that we attribute to the objects in everyday life? In an influential study that came out in 1947, the Dartmouth professor Rudolf Luneburg proposed that human vision is organized according to the principles of hyperbolic, non-Euclidean geometry.[7] These terms require some explanation. Euclid was a Greek mathematician who lived in the third century BCE. In his work *Elements* he summarized the entire knowledge of geometry in his time. Euclid's approach was to start from some very simple and obvious truths (or postulates), for instance, that all right angles are equal, and then show how complex geometrical theorems can be proved starting from such simple assumptions. The fifth postulate in his list was, however, neither obvious nor simple. It said that if a line intersects two other lines, and if the sum of the intersection angles on one side is less than two right angles, then the two lines would meet on that side. Mathematically, this is equivalent to saying that if you have a line and a point outside the line, you can draw only one line through that point parallel with the given line.

For centuries, mathematicians debated whether it was necessary to include this fifth postulate in the list of elementary geometrical truths. They wondered whether it was possible to prove it somehow, starting from the remaining postulates. In the nineteenth century, the Russian mathematician Nikolay Lobachevsky tried to do this by assuming that it was possible to draw *more* than one line through a given point parallel with a given line. He was hoping that this would produce a theorem that would be absurd and contradict the remaining elementary geometrical postulates. In that case he would have proved that the fifth postulate depends on other postulates. But this did not happen—rather, he developed a different, *hyperbolic*, geometry. His theorems described a different kind of space than the one in which we live. Such a space is characterized by a different geometry in which, for instance, the sum of the angles of a triangle is less than 180 degrees.

Subsequently, following his steps other mathematicians discovered other geometries by reformulating Euclid's postulates. Such geometries (and the spaces they describe) are called non-Euclidean. While these geometries are very different from the geometry of the world that we know and inhabit, they have found wide application in physics. But they are not applicable in our everyday life or architecture— the geometry of the world we inhabit is Euclidean. (There are architects who will try to impress their colleagues and the general public by saying that they have designed a non-Euclidean house. Such claims are nonsense: in such a house, for instance, there would have to be *more than one line* going through the upper corner of the window that is at the same time parallel with the sill.)[8]

While we live our everyday lives in Euclidean space, and while Euclidean geometry is the geometry of the light rays that reach our eyes, it is nevertheless not necessary to assume that the geometry of the human experience of space must follow the postulates of Euclidean geometry. This was precisely Rudolf Luneburg's assumption— he argued that our visual experience is organized according to the principles of a non-Euclidean, hyperbolic geometry, such as the one originally described by Lobachevsky. The phenomenon of constancies, which was described in the previous chapter, is a very strong reason to think that our visual experience does not conform to Euclidean geometry. If it did, then it would be fully consistent with the geometry of light and consequently the laws of perspective. But as mentioned above, many people, for instance, perceive that a person approaching them retains the same size.

Consequently, following Luneburg, in the second half of the twentieth century a number of attempts were made to show that the geometry of human visual experience conforms to some type of non-Euclidean geometry known to mathematicians.[9] In other words, psychological experiments show that there can be systematic mismatches (such as constancies) between physical space and the human visual experience of that space. The idea is then to determine which geometry, known in mathematics, is best at explaining the mismatches that have been discovered. Mark Wagner, who has summarized these attempts in a recent book, has called this approach *synthetic*. Following such an approach, scientists are striving to establish which geometrical postulates best explain the results of specific psychological experiments and then assume that such geometry will always work. However, writing sixty years after Luneburg, Wagner observed that these attempts have systematically failed, and that subsequent empirical research has refuted them.[10] In his view, there is no single geometry of visual space, but many; they vary with mental set, experience, conditions, and time.[11] In opposition to the synthetic approach, he suggests an *analytic* approach, one that does not impose on human vision a body of geometrical postulates but, rather, tries to determine the measurable properties of visual space, such as distances, locations, areas, and psychological factors. According to this view, the daily space in which we live is Euclidean, the architecture we build has to be Euclidean, but the way we perceive it is not describable by a single geometrical system, and a great variety of factors may affect human visual experience.

VISUAL IMAGINATION

Perceiving things in space, however, cannot be the same as *thinking about* their spatial properties. Insofar as our perception is not organized according to the principles of Euclidean space, we would not be able to survive in the Euclidean everyday space we inhabit if we were not able to figure out somehow the real geometry and spatial disposition of things. Even if our perception is not Euclidean, we must possess some methods to grasp what things really are like in order to orient ourselves and move in the world we inhabit.

When spatial thinking is mentioned, one's first association is visual imagination. As noted in the second chapter, during the middle decades of the twentieth century behaviorist approaches to psychology suppressed research on visual imagination. Before that, however, some very interesting research on visual imagination was underway in American psychology. In an experiment that later became famous, Cheves West Perky showed his subjects slides of various everyday objects (e.g., vegetables) projected on a smoked-screen glass.[12] The brightness of these pictures was adjusted so that they were barely perceptible. The pictures were also deliberately made fuzzy. The subjects, who were not aware that any kind of pictures were being shown to them, were invited to imagine objects of their choice while looking at the screen. Typically, they reported imagining the very object they were being shown on the screen. The implication would be that in some cases the distinction between mental imagery and the perception of an external object is uncertain.

The rise of behaviorism brought an end to research on visual imagination; behaviorists regarded the topic as unscientific. It was the important experiments on imagination by Roger Shepard that signaled, in the 1970s, the demise of behaviorism in American psychology.[13] Shepard showed his subjects pictures of the combinations of ten cubes aligned in different ways and pictured from different sides, similar to those presented in figure 16. The groups of cubes were shown from different sides as if they had been rotated in space. The subjects were asked to say whether various pictures showed the same or different combinations of cubes. The task itself was easy. With a little practice the subjects were able to achieve accuracy that closely approached 100 percent. What mattered to the experimenters, however, was the time the subjects needed to respond. The images showed combinations of cubes rotated from 0 to 180 degrees. As it turned out, the bigger the angle, the more time the subjects needed for their responses. The time needed for mental rotation turned out to be proportional to the angle of the rotation.[14] When describing how they reached their answer, the subjects reported that they were rotating mental images in their imagination in order to solve the problem. All this meant that visual imagination was not something psychologists could easily dismiss. (It is interesting to note that two other psychologists, Valerie Hollard and Jean Delius, managed to train pigeons to solve the same spatial problem as successfully as humans—but in the case of pigeons, there was no correlation between the angle of rotation and answering time. It is therefore believed that pigeons do not rely on mental imagery.)[15]

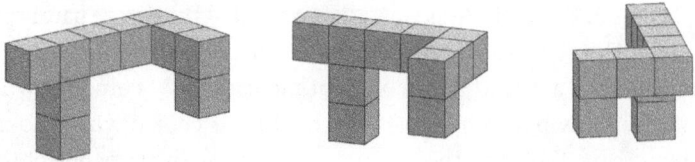

16 Drawings that show one and the same cluster of cubes from different sides were used by Roger Shepard to test mental rotation.

In another, similar experiment, Shepard showed his subjects letters and numbers (e.g., the letter R) rotated at different angles. The subjects were asked whether the images they were shown were made by rotating the letter R or its mirror image. Once again, it turned out that the time the subjects needed to respond was proportional to the angle of rotation. Shepard also asked his subjects to compare pairs of US states according to their geometrical similarity without looking at a map—and they were able to do this reasonably well. The fact that such mental comparisons are possible shows that it is possible to make judgments about shapes without looking at them.

Another important contribution to the debate about visual imagery during the 1970s was Allan Paivio's *dual coding* theory.[16] Paivio argued that the human mind stores information in two different ways, by verbal coding and pictorial representations. Basically, in his view, the human mind operates with two interconnected memory systems, one verbal and another visual. The implication was that some thinking was verbal, some visual, and the latter could not be reduced to the former.

Shepard's experiments and Paivio's arguments triggered a particularly vehement dispute between those psychologists who affirmed and those who denied the existence of human visual imagination. Philosophers were also very quick to join the fray. In the early 1980s, the debate was marked by the passion with which participants took sides in favor or against mental imagery. The level of passion was often quite inappropriate for a scientific or philosophical debate.[17] The American philosopher Daniel Dennett, who often defended positions aligned with behaviorism, attempted to argue that the products of visual imagination are more like verbal descriptions than like pictures, but these arguments have not fared well in subsequent debate.[18] Dennett argued that if an image is to function as an image, someone must observe it, so an image in the mind would require another person to observe it, and so on ad infinitum. (In philosophy of mind this argument is sometimes called "the homunculus argument.") In his view, the last image in the process of perception is the retinal image. This argument was refuted by another philosopher, Jerry Fodor.[19] Fodor pointed out that Dennett's argument assumes that if recovering information from the external environment requires an image, then recovering information from an image must also require an image. It is, however, not clear that we need to make this assumption.

Dennett further argued that when describing a person in words one need not mention whether the person is wearing a hat—and similarly, when imagining a person one can also avoid that issue. In Dennett's view, this shows that imagining is more similar to a verbal description than to a picture. Similarly, if the products of imagination were like pictures, then imagining a tiger would mean imagining a definite number of stripes. But people who say that they are imagining a tiger often cannot immediately say how many stripes they have imagined on the tiger. However, Fodor pointed out that these arguments merely show that in some situations mental images are not fully determinate.

EXPLAINING VISUAL IMAGINATION

Human brains certainly do not construct physical models of things we imagine and then rotate them: when a person imagines a car, there is no physical three-dimensional model of a car in the brain itself. No physical model is rotated in the brain in order to see what a thing looks like from different sides. Nor is there a physical picture in the brain of the thing imagined. Whatever the mental mechanism that enables us to imagine visually, it is important to ask whether we actually *think* using images, or do we think and then merely represent our thoughts to ourselves using visual imagination. Is our visual imagination merely an interface or part of our thinking mechanisms?

An important proponent of the former thesis—that the brain actually thinks by forming images—was Stephen Kosslyn.[20] Kosslyn and his team assumed that imagination is comparable to the cathode ray tube in the TV sets used at the time, in the 1970s. They conceived of images as temporary spatial displays in active memory generated from representations in long-term memory. The system makes information from long-term memory explicit in an image; pictorial properties of imagery are functional and not merely representations of thoughts. When thinking about spatial objects, we are *depicting* them to ourselves, not describing them. "Depiction" here means that, in principle, every portion of the representation corresponds to a portion of the represented object; human spatial thinking is then analog.

Starting from this assumption, Kosslyn formulated a series of experiments about human visualization. For instance, he showed his subjects a map of an island with twenty-one objects on the map and asked them to memorize it. The subjects were then given the name of an object and asked to look for it on the map as they remembered it. They were to scan to the object and push a button when reaching it, if the object was on the map at all. As it turned out, the longer the distance between objects, the more time the subjects needed to get to specific objects. Another group of subjects was also shown the map. However, they were told that after imaging the map they were simply to decide whether or not the probe word named an object on the map. In this case, distance between objects in the map had no effect on the time they needed to decide. When conducting these experiments, Kosslyn did not intend to suggest that people actually have television screens in their heads.[21] Rather, in his view, although mental images may lack physical spatial characteristics (we don't have physical pictures in our heads), they nonetheless function as if they had them. One can say that mental images are not really in space (we don't have actual pictures in our brains) but they are in a medium that *functions* like spatial representations.

Another American psychologist, Zenon Pylyshyn, developed an extensive critique of Kosslyn's approach to visual imagery.[22] Pylyshyn saw in Kosslyn's approach a tendency to confuse reporting about the properties of the objects that people imagine and the actual properties of the image. He pointed out that Kosslyn in his writing easily transforms a statement such as "these results seem to indicate that images do represent metrical distance" into the assertion that "images have spatial extent." In Pylyshyn's view, mental rotation is to be explained as a manifestation of *tacit knowledge*. Tacit knowledge is a kind of knowledge that one assumes even when one is not consciously aware of it. One may even not know how to express such knowledge in words. In an experiment Pylyshyn instructed his subjects to imagine moving around a figure drawn on the floor of a room. Some of them reported that they could not do it, because the movement they imagined brought them against the wall. In other words, their tacit (implicit) knowledge of the shape of the room affected their ability to imagine moving in a certain direction. Pylyshyn gives numerous examples of tacit knowledge. For instance, imagine rotating the letter C counterclockwise by 90 degrees. It suddenly appears to have the shape of the letter U. Or, imagine a square with a dot in it. Then imagine the width of the square being elongated until it becomes a wide rectangle. The dot will still be inside the figure. Or, imagine writing the letters A through E on a piece of paper. In this case, one will imagine that the letter D is to the right of the letter B. In none of these examples is one aware of the reasoning that produces these results.

In Pylyshyn's view, something similar happens when we use visual imagination to solve geometrical problems. Geometrical problems can be solved this way because visual imagination relies on our tacit knowledge of physical processes. Imagine dropping two balls of identical shape but different weight. Which ball do you imagine will hit the ground first? Those who know from physics that heavier bodies do not fall faster will imagine them falling at the same time; other people may imagine that the heavier ball falls faster. Or, imagine a yellow and a blue light filter. Now imagine that the two filters are moved so that they overlap. Which color do you see through the superimposed filters? Answering such questions means relying on our tacit knowledge of physical processes. In Pylyshyn's view, the same happens in the case of spatial mental rotation. The knowledge of natural laws of this kind is not inborn; rather, it results from the fact that our imagination depends on our tacit knowledge. In Kosslyn's scanning experiment, it is possible that the subjects were merely reproducing the process they believed they needed to generate, because the instructions suggested that this was the aim of the experiment.

In his response to Pylyshyn's criticism, Kosslyn agreed that in some cases our tacit knowledge affects our imagination—for instance, in the case of mixing light filters or dropping balls.[23] However, in his view, visual imagining that relies on the knowledge of physical laws should not be confused with the examples that depend on the knowledge of geometry. Kosslyn's response is credible; there seem to exist good reasons to insist on the distinction between the use of geometrical (spatial) and physical laws in imagination. I can decide to imagine that the yellow and blue filters in the above example are a special kind of filter that, when placed one over another, produce red color. In this case, I will indeed be able to imagine seeing red through the combination of these two filters. But this does not work with geometrical properties. I cannot imagine a special kind of a sphere whose intersection with a plane would be a triangle. The imagination of geometrical properties is not penetrable by our decisions as is the case with our imagination of other physical properties.

DOLPHINS, BATS, AND ARCHITECTS

Psychologists' debates about visual imagination ultimately show that our thinking about spatial properties has to be visual. When we think about spatial objects that we are not perceiving, we have to engage our *visual* imagination. In recent years, some architectural theorists, such as Juhani Pallasmaa, have discussed, with enthusiasm, nonvisual ways to think about architecture's spatial properties. Pallasmaa talks about the acoustic experience of space: "the acoustic harshness of an uninhabited and unfurnished house as compared to the affability of a lived home, in which sound is refracted and softened by the surfaces of numerous objects of personal life."[24] He also says that for him the strongest memories of some places are those of odor.[25] Such examples, however, merely illustrate how poor and incomplete our awareness of architectural works must be when it is constructed to exclude their visual properties.[26] Some smells and noises certainly can be associated with some buildings—but we can know only very little about buildings, their spaces, shapes, and colors, when we base our knowledge purely on accidental smells or sounds. Architectural works have many properties that are not visual, but once their visual aspects are disregarded, we are left with a very paltry idea about their spatial qualities.

Some animals can indeed deal with space successfully without relying on vision. Dolphins and bats explore the world around them using echolocation. They produce noises that objects reflect. On the basis of the echoes they receive, their brains can determine the distance, position, size, shape, motion, texture, and hardness of things that the echo comes from.[27] It would be interesting to know whether they can also imagine sounds that would come from objects that are not present. Maybe they even have the capacity for sound-based mental rotation. Maybe they can imagine how an object would sound if it rotated and was heard from different sides. But even if bats and dolphins can do it, humans certainly cannot. Our experience of spatial objects is fundamentally based on sight. Humans who lose their sight have serious problems in everyday life; they cannot just switch to echolocation or smells. Even when we are not directly looking at things, the most efficient way to contemplate their spatial properties is by *visual* imagination. The point is not that someone wants to ban sounds or smells from architecture. The point is that, for humans, sounds and smells are of little use when it comes to defining the spatial properties of architectural works. (Just imagine an architect who provided builders, not with plans of the building they are expected to build, but rather with samples of smells intended to "define" the building's spatial properties.) Consequently, the more importance one ascribes to the spatial properties of architectural works, the less one will be inclined to pay attention to smells or sounds. The same applies to tactile properties. By touching small things we can get an idea about their shape—but the idea that one can get about a major internal space by merely touching the walls of the building is not going to be a comprehensive one.

On a more profound level, however, Pallasmaa does make an important point when he complains that in our present situation "architecture has turned into an art form of instant visual image."[28] This complaint cannot pertain to our theoretical understanding of architecture, since architectural theory, for reasons described in the first two chapters, has been programmatically anti-visual for decades; Pallasmaa's own writings belong to this genre as well.[29] But it is true that the emphasis on narratives has produced a culture in which narratives associated with buildings are often illustrated, in publications, with powerful images. These images are indeed often selected for the instantaneous impact they can make; their purpose is to illustrate visually a certain narrative. Pallasmaa is right when he says that we are left with the use of "retinal images for the purpose of immediate persuasion."[30] Illustrations in contemporary architectural publications often provide very little information about buildings' three-dimensional, spatial qualities. The problem is best seen in current architectural publishing. Professional journals hardly ever publish plans of buildings. The same applies to architectural books coming off the presses these days. The emphasis on narratives generates a visuality that replaces interest in the spatial properties of buildings with images that are attractive illustrations of specific narratives. If architecture's visuality is to regain architecture's spatial component, we need an understanding of architecture in which its three-dimensional properties matter—in which architectural works are not reduced to mere objects stories can be told about.

MENTAL ROTATION, 3-D MODELING, AND DESCRIPTIVE GEOMETRY

To an architect, these discussions of the visual nature of architecture's spatiality give much to ponder about. Three-dimensional thinking is the core skill in architectural work. Although the "Mental Rotation" article in *Wikipedia* states that Roger Shepard and Jacqueline Metzler, the psychologists who first made experiments about mental rotation, discovered this phenomenon,[31] the authors of the article should have known better: the very idea of representing buildings in plan, section, and elevation assumes the ability to imagine architectural works from different sides. For instance, a drawing from 1570 by the architect Andrea Palladio shows the details of the Ionic order shown from different sides. (See fig. 17.) By reading this drawing, stonemasons could grasp what the elements of the Ionic order should look like and then make them. Obviously, modern CAD programs are a means to perform spatial rotation on a screen with greater accuracy than visual imagination can achieve. The discipline of descriptive geometry, which used to be extensively taught in architecture schools, involved the skill of geometrically constructing views of objects from different sides. The skill was used to solve the geometrical problems that arise in everyday architectural design before computers started being used for the purpose—for instance, to determine the line of intersection of two curved ceilings (such as vaults). There exists a body of research showing that teaching such geometrical skills to young architects is useful because it develops their ability to think spatially.[32]

If we are going to talk about the aesthetic qualities of architectural works, we need to be aware that these works are going to be thought about not only as perceived from a single point in space but as three-dimensional objects. We perceive a building from one side, from another, from inside, we observe the composition of spaces, and after some time we have formed a comprehensive understanding of

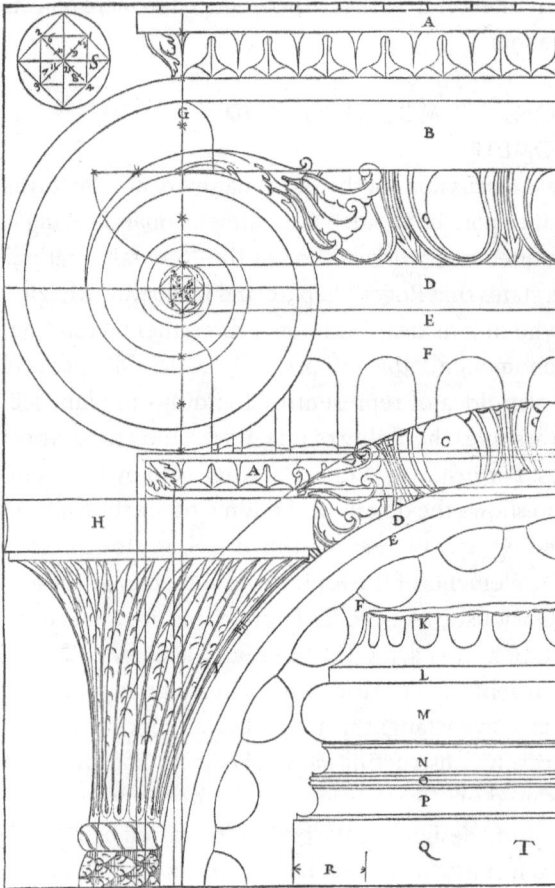

17 Detail of the Ionic order from Andrea Palladio, *Four Books on Architecture*

the building's three-dimensionality. Or, we don't have to be dealing with a built building at all; we can grasp its spatial qualities by studying its plans, sections, and elevations. By analogy with 3-D computer modeling, one could say that we have formulated a 3-D mental model of the building in our minds.[33] Obviously, buildings can also be attributed some aesthetic properties on the basis of the way we observe them from a certain point in space—for instance, the way they fit the ensemble of a square as perceived from a particular direction. But it may be argued that such qualities belong to the art of stage design, rather than architecture proper.

There is also the question of whether we attribute aesthetic properties to architectural works as physical objects or on the basis of spaces they form. Among architectural theorists, it was August Schmarsow who famously insisted that architects design spaces, not buildings. In his view, buildings are "spatial constructs, whatever their material, duration or construction."[34] Architecture students in their early years typically think that they are designing buildings, physical objects, and this attitude manifests itself in designs with "leaking" and "leftover" spaces. Some architects, in fact, continue designing buildings as physical objects for the rest of their lives. But many students, in their third or fourth year of studies, switch to thinking about the spaces they design; the building becomes the shell that serves to form

18 San Lorenzo, Turin, Guarino Guarini

these spaces. Nevertheless, it would be excessive to say that the shell is irrelevant. One still certainly has to consider the aesthetic impact of the surfaces that form it, their color and texture. Spatial design is about considering the space the building forms as the negative of the building itself. Nevertheless, one could hardly say that the great quality of an elaborate dome, such as the one in Guarino Guarini's Church of San Lorenzo in Turin, is the negative space that its ornamentation forms. (See fig. 18.) Architectural aesthetic qualities belong both to a building and to the spaces it forms.

5

THE RETURN OF THE VISUAL

We have seen that the idea that architectural works can be evaluated only in relation to the ideas associated with them, the stories that can be told about them, became influential in the 1960s, as a result of then-current breakthroughs in philosophy and the psychology of perception. But these disciplines did not stop developing in the 1960s. Arguably, the major problem in our contemporary understanding of architecture is that architectural theory has not kept pace with developments in those fields.

NONCONCEPTUAL CONTENT

There is some irony in the fact that in the late 1980s and the 1990s, precisely the period in which conceptualism became so dominant in the understanding of architecture, the idea that perception is insepa-rable from conceptualization lost its credibility among philosophers and psychologists. This was largely due to new research about the nonconceptual content and the impenetrability of human visual processes. The demise of the view that all perception is conceptual happened concurrently with the demise of the idea that all thinking is verbal. While this latter idea still underlies much of contemporary thinking about architecture, during the 1990s it lost its psychological and philosophical credibility as a result of a wave of research about the mental process of animals and children before they have mastered a language. If we accept that animals think, then we cannot argue that all thinking is in a language. In any case, it took reasonably sophisti-cated psychological research in the 1990s to point out that animals and children are capable of thought before learning a language.

The idea that vision is inseparable from classification was problem-atic for philosophers even at the time when it was widely accepted. It implies that only that which can be classified can be perceived; that the things one cannot classify, one cannot perceive.[1] However, if we do not perceive things and properties that we have not encountered in the past, we cannot learn to classify or see them. So one problematic implication of this view is that, starting from birth, we cannot learn to see new things or properties. The first systematic philosophical attempt to articulate an opposition to the view that perception is inseparable from concepts and beliefs was Fred Dretske's 1969 book *Seeing and Knowing*. Dretske argued that there is a primitive visual ability that we share with a "cocker spaniel or a pet cat." For instance, people can see maple trees without thinking that they see a tree or even a physical object. A statement that people sometimes make, "I do not know whether I really saw something or I imagined it," is a good example of a state of mind in which perception is not accompanied by any identifying belief. Or, imagine an officer saluting a company of passing soldiers. It is hard to think that what the company's dog mascot saw depended on the dog's beliefs, if he had any: rather it depended on the excellence of his eyes, the distance of the men, and so on.

Dretske's articulation of the view that perception can have content that need not depend on the previous knowledge, beliefs, or concepts we operate with resulted in an industry of research in the philosophy of perception during the late 1980s and through the 1990s. The idea that it is possible to perceive without classifying or conceptualizing what one sees—that perception can have content independently of our concepts—came to be known as the argument about "nonconceptual content."[2] One important group of arguments about nonconceptual content pertains to the fact that human perception and its contents are much richer than the conceptual frameworks human beings operate with.[3] The number of nuances of the same color that a human eye can differentiate by far exceeds the available concepts, let alone our abilities to name all these colors. Those philosophers who argued that the contents of perception are independent of concepts we operate with pointed out that perception is more *fine-grained* than available conceptual frameworks. For instance, if one looks at a range of mountains, some sections of the range can be called rounded, others jagged.[4] However, the content of that visual experience in respect to the shape of the mountains is far more specific than a verbal description can indicate. Similarly, the symmetry of an inkblot can be perceived by someone who does not have the concept of symmetry.

It is this same argument about the fine-grained nature of human vision that the student in the review described in the first chapter pondered on when she doubted that Derrida could help her make design decisions about color or the shape of a window. The response that modern philosophical research would give to this dilemma is the same as hers: philosophical theories can provide conceptual frameworks, but these frameworks are always going to be insufficient to describe, let alone decide about, visual, spatial, and formal properties of architectural works. Consider for instance the column studies by the Zurich architect Michael Hansmeyer—no amount of storytelling can decide about such complex forms. (See fig. 19.) The architect's

19 Column study, Michael Hansmeyer

formal decision ultimately has to be based on visual judgment. We can now also see why the introduction of digital media into architecture resulted in increased formalist inclinations among architects. The use of digital media has allowed unprecedented formal complexities in design. At the same time, the fine-grained nature of human visuality that Dretske talked about makes it impossible to base all the necessary design decisions on stories, narratives, or symbolism. Simply, there are too many formal decisions to be made and no amount of story-telling will help do that. The only procedure architects can rely on is their visual judgment. The levels of formal complexity that the digital revolution has enabled had to result in an emphasis on visual-formal judgments.

Another important argument about nonconceptual perception came from the philosopher Tim Crane.[5] Crane observed that a person cannot have contradictory beliefs—for instance, genuinely be-

20 Busan Opera House Competition, South Korea, 2011, Florencia Pita FPMO

lieve that a thing is moving and staying still at the same time. It follows that when things are perceived to move and stand still, we must be perceiving them independently of our beliefs. Crane then points out that this indeed happens if one stares for a period of time at a scene that contains movement in one direction, and then looks at a scene that contains no movement. In this latter scene the objects will appear to move in the opposite direction to that of the original movement, while at the same time they will not appear to move relative to other objects in the scene. The situation happens if one stares at a waterfall and then turns one's sight to some stationary object. The stationary object will appear to move, although not relative to its background. Our perception then depicts an object that moves and stays still at the same time. But in that case it cannot derive from (depend on) what we believe that we see, since in that case we would have contradictory beliefs.

Research on nonconceptual content is important for philosophers because it helps differentiate between *individuating* and *identifying* an object. Athanassios Raftopoulos in his 2009 book *Cognition and Perception* summarized this discussion by saying that the important aspect of nonconceptual content is that it enables individuating, but not identifying, the objects of perception.[6] The philosophers' point is that if all perception were conceptually driven it would be difficult to explain how objects can be individuated in perception.[7] (This is the difference between seeing that something is in front of us and identifying it.) Insofar as the concept according to which an object is perceived is a set of classificatory criteria, it is hard to explain how we can know that something remains the same object after some of its properties change. After a change, the object would be identified by another concept—and it would be impossible to perceive it as the same object with new properties. If nonclassificatory perception were impossible, we could not say when we are dealing with the same thing after the thing changes some of its properties. For instance, a lightbulb starts shining after I turn the power on. Since "shining lightbulb" and "non-shining lightbulb" are different concepts, I would be subsuming the lightbulb under different concepts before and after turning the light on. But if we assume that all perception is strictly conceptual, I would not be able to say that it is the same lightbulb that started shining when I turned the light on. This problem is easily solved if we can nonconceptually individuate objects in perception. At the same time, a substantial body of psychological research also indicates that we individuate objects (for instance, when tracking their movement) without relying on our conceptual knowledge about these objects.[8] Philosophical literature on nonconceptual content is full of examples that may appear as hair splitting to nonphilosophers, but they ultimately support the understanding that perception can be independent of the concepts under which we subsume the objects we perceive.

IMPENETRABILITY OF VISION

An important stream of research in psychology over the past twenty years pertains to the differentiation between *sense* perception and *cognitive* perception.[9] The former is assumed to be concept-independent. We have seen in the previous chapter that in the early 1980s the psychologist David Marr introduced research on "early vision" as separate from the study of the cognitive aspects of visual perception.[10] This research concentrated on analyzing the various sensory dimensions of perceptual experience, such as shape, color, size, distance, and so on. In contrast to "early vision," one could talk about "late vision," which would be equivalent to cognitive perception that concerns recognizing, identifying, or classifying.[11]

In a highly influential paper that came out in 1999, the psychologist Zenon Pylyshyn argued that early vision is impenetrable to conceptual thinking.[12] In his view, vision is to be understood as a complex information-processing system.[13] "Early vision" is one of its sections; it computes the spatial three-dimensional layout of visible objects in the perceived scene. It enables us to grasp the spatial dispositions and shapes of objects we perceive visually. However, it does not relate what we see to the things we have seen before. It has no access to the contents of our memory. It is independent of other beliefs we may have, previous experience or cultural influences. Thus conceived, early vision is part of the hardwire of our visual system and a result of the evolution of the human species.

The arguments that Pylyshyn presented in support of this view can be grouped into a number of different categories. In the past, perceptual illusions were typically used by the proponents of New Look psychology to show how malleable our perception is and how it is largely influenced by our expectations. Fraser's spiral, for instance, consists of concentric circles that are perceived as a spiral. (See fig. 21. Tracing the spiral with a pencil will show that these are indeed circles

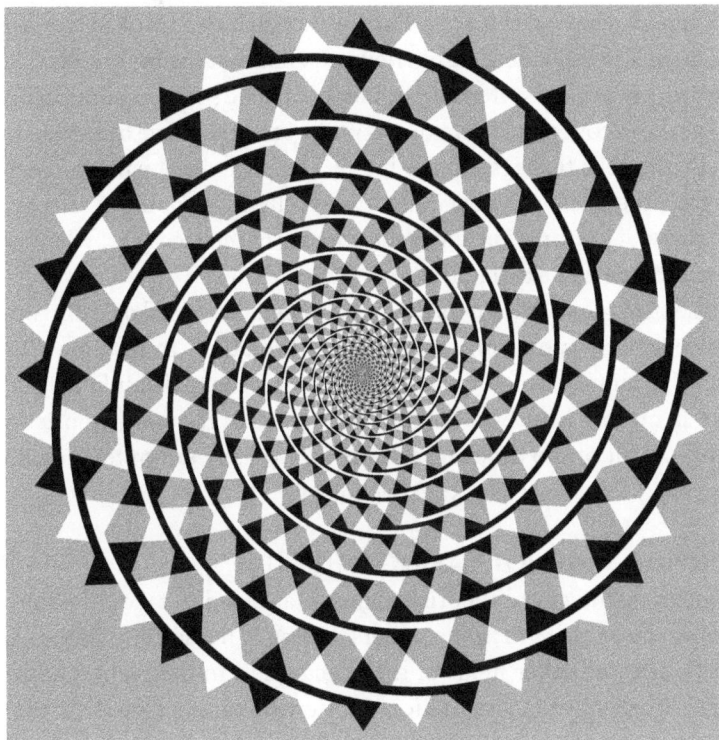

21 Fraser spiral

and not a spiral.) The 1950s New Look interpretation would be that in such cases our eyes are misled by our expectations. But Pylyshyn's response is that even when we *know* that we are looking at an optical illusion, we still perceive the illusion.[14] The conclusion is that our perception is independent of our beliefs and knowledge. Pylyshyn also pointed out that there are certain types of brain damage (visual agnosia) in which the patients are able to see things as shapes and spatial objects, but are not able to recognize conceptually what they are.[15] Such patients can see, but (e.g., as a result of a stroke) cannot recognize familiar objects or faces. They cannot tell what the object is, but they can describe its spatial features. This also indicates that the part of brain that deals with visual and spatial properties is separate from conceptual thinking. Finally, Pylyshyn also invoked the fact that there is little evidence from neuroscience that the brain cells that constitute the visual system are influenced by the sections of the brain that perform conceptual thinking.[16] While scientists have been able to specify the cells that respond to highly complex visual patterns such as a face, there is no evidence that these cells' functioning is affected by nonvisual information about the identity of the face (e.g., whether a specific face was expected in a certain situation).

The strength of Pylyshyn's thesis was that it was based on extensive knowledge of the existing experimental literature. In his view, the belief that human perception depends on conceptual thinking, that there is no innocent eye, is really a product of the mid-twentieth-century spirit of the time and faith in biologically unlimited human potential.[17] It belongs to 1950s psychology.

ENJOYING AND NOT CARING WHAT IT IS

Although architectural theorists have so far failed to take them into account, these changes in the understanding of human visuality have already affected other fields of the humanities. In the realm of analytic, English-speaking aesthetics, the view that human vision is permeated by conceptual thinking largely became dominant as a result of the publication of Kendall Walton's 1970 paper "Categories of Art."

The article was strongly influenced by Gombrich's view that perception is relative to the categories in which one sees. Walton's argument
was that, for instance, the energy or brilliance of a fast section in a vio-
lin concert derives not only from the absolute speed of the music but
also from the fact that it is fast for that particular medium. Similarly,
one may regard cubist paintings or Chinese music as formless on the
first contact, because one is not perceiving them as cubist paintings
or Chinese music. The conclusion that remained very influential for a
number of decades was that aesthetic properties are always attributed
in accordance with the category of that specific work of art. In Walton's view, if we excavated an artwork from the dust of an archaeologi-
cal site on Mars, we would not be able to attribute to it any aesthetic
properties, since we would know nothing about the civilization that
created it and we would not know how to categorize it. The idea is
that we could not like its shapes or proportions (Gombrich would say,
even perceive) independently of what we know or don't know about
its origin.

Subsequent developments in philosophy and psychology had enabled a full rejection of this view by the late 1990s. The central figure
in the formalist revolution in aesthetics has been the British aesthe-
tician Nick Zangwill. In a series of papers Zangwill has argued for
a *moderate formalist* position—that is, the view that some aesthetic
properties depend exclusively on formal properties of objects, while
others depend on nonformal properties as well.[18] Zangwill's point was
that Walton never demonstrated that no aesthetic properties could be
attributed to works of art purely on the basis of their formal properties. In the context of architecture, it is not unreasonable to understand Zangwill's "formal" properties as those that would be processed
by "early vision": shapes and the spatial layout of things.[19] In that case
he would be saying that some aesthetic judgments can be based on
nonconceptual visual processing. For instance, it could be argued that
we can enjoy certain shapes by perceiving them independently of the
concepts that we associate with them. Obviously, in his time, Walton
was able to assume that no formal properties could be perceived inde-

pendently of concepts attributed to them. Consequently, if perception is inseparable from categorization, the attribution of aesthetic properties must be too. Zangwill clearly could not have credibly argued his position in the 1970s. If the dominant view is that there is no perception without classification, then it becomes hard to claim convincingly that some aesthetic properties can be attributed independently of how we classify the objects that we attribute these properties to. How could we make such attributions if nothing can be perceived without being classified and categorized? But this reasoning ceases to be credible once it is assumed that one can perceive without categorizing.

It is hard to imagine that our understanding of architecture can remain unaffected by the revolution in the scientific and philosophical explanations of human vision that has happened in the past twenty years. If architectural works can be perceived and thought about visually, independently of the beliefs or stories we associate with them, it becomes hard to explain why we should care about the meanings some people may attribute to them. Pure visual aesthetic preference becomes (again) a valid topic in its own right. In architectural studio teaching, privileging narratives over visual and spatial considerations becomes merely a sign of an old-fashioned bias. Many other twentieth-century architectural dogmas are also bound to lose credibility. Consider the belief that all architecture has to be appropriate to its time. Appropriateness to time is ultimately a concept that is attached to some architectural works, but denied to others. If one says that architecture has to be appropriate to its time, one is also saying that no architecture can be appreciated independently of concepts associated with it. Antiformalism of this kind has been the original sin of modernist architecture since its inception. It is now time to lay such reasoning to rest.

BACK TO THE STUDIO

For architects, Zangwill's moderate formalism helps resolve many dilemmas. It answers radical conceptualist arguments while avoiding the pitfall of extreme formalism—the reduction of all architectural concerns to purely visual issues. Certainly, there are functional and structural issues that architects must deal with, and this can be done only through conceptual thinking. Certainly, an architectural work culturally interacts with the community in which it is placed, and this interaction is largely based on how the community interprets and conceptualizes the architectural work. But this is not all of it, and Zangwill's moderate formalism provides the grounds to regard formal, visual, and spatial issues as architects' legitimate concerns.

The studio situation described at the beginning of the first chapter illustrates the kind of architectural interests that Zangwill's arguments make legitimate. From this perspective, the visual interests of the student who presented her work are perfectly appropriate, while her professors' obstinate refusal to consider them can only be defended by relying on philosophical and psychological positions that have long lost their currency. In a situation where it is recognized that architectural works can be perceived, imagined, thought about, mentally rotated, and that their geometries can be studied, their colors discussed, and so on, *independently of any concepts or meanings we associate with these works,* only an ideologically biased professor can insist on evaluating the work exclusively on the basis of the story that can be told about it.

These are, however, intellectual reasons to defend a (moderate) formalist position in contemporary architectural practice and studio teaching. In reality, there will always be architects, studio professors, or architecture students who are more interested in the visual, spatial, and formal properties of architectural works—and those who insist on the stories that can be told about such works. For the latter, the views of the former are simply not appropriately intellectual for academia (presumably, academia should be intellectual); for the former, the pseudointellectualism of the latter is merely a sign of creative incapacity inappropriate for a creative field like architecture. Consider what happens if a formalist student is paired with a conceptualist professor, or vice versa. The conceptualist professor will expect a narrative and more than a "mere form" from the student.

As a result, the formalist student will design a building and then feel forced to concoct a story in order to please the professor. In such situations, students quickly become cynical, since they know they are being awarded grades for producing fake stories about their design process and motivation. As a result, architectural education becomes an exercise in intellectual dishonesty. But the situation is not happier if, vice versa, a conceptualist student is paired with a formalist professor. The student will believe that the professor's emphasis on visual issues is missing something important. The professor will see in the student's attempts to motivate design using concepts associated with the work a silly evasion from real design work at best, or radical lack of creative talent at worst.

In one sense, however, both formalists and conceptualists are in the same boat. The question of the validity of their preferences affects them both in the same way. How can one evaluate architectural works on the basis of their spatial and visual properties if such judgments are relative to individuals?

Alternatively, how can one evaluate architectural works on the basis of the conceptual contents and narratives associated with them, considering that preference for various narratives or conceptual contents is relative to individuals? Can we expect people to agree about aesthetic judgments, visual or conceptual? If not, what is, for instance, the meaning of the grade component awarded for the aesthetic aspects of a student's work in an architecture studio? How can one grade students' work on the basis of aesthetic judgments if aesthetic judgments are relative to individuals? A comparison with mathematics can resolve some confusion. Few people would argue that mathematics is relative to individuals—but also, few people would deny that the ability to make judgments about mathematics differs from person to person. High-level mathematical competence is a rare skill. Nevertheless, we do not say that *mathematics itself* is relative to individuals; we say that mathematical skills are relative to individuals. This is not merely because it is possible to state proofs of mathematical theorems: again, few people can grasp these proofs anyhow. The point is that the physical laws according to which the world operates are mathematical. A physicist who thought that mathematics was arbitrary would not get very far with his or her experiments; an engineer who assumed that mathematics was a matter of his or her whims would be soon out of job. Mathematics is an aspect of the real world—while aesthetic judgments are not. They are about individual human preferences, and statements about preferences cannot be checked against anything in the physical world. People can lie, because they are deceiving themselves or because they want to impress their peers; they may be genuinely unable to make aesthetic judgments (the way many people are when it comes to mathematics) but do not want to admit it. The problem is not that the ability to make aesthetic judgments is relative to individuals (this is the case with all human skills); the problem is that mental states that motivate the statements expressing such judgments cannot be checked. At the same time, these statements are precisely about mental states, the individual's aesthetic reaction. Ultimately, the same problem applies to any field where one has to rely on the judgment of experts—aesthetic judgments in architecture are not different than judgments in other fields.

Once we accept this, then we can also ask, what is it that makes certain aesthetic judgments possible for certain individuals? Here too Zangwill's moderate formalism shows important strengths. If the attribution of *some* aesthetic properties is independent of concepts, beliefs, or knowledge about individual works of art, then such properties are going to be more general and more widely accessible than those properties whose attribution depends on conceptual thinking. Since concepts are acquired through interaction within a specific community, Walton-style emphasis on the aesthetic properties that depend on conceptual thinking turns out to be a mere celebration of cultural parochialism. Zangwill may not be saying that nonconceptual judgments are universally valid for all humans—after all, there may be people who are incapable of aesthetic judgments the way some people are blind to colors. But he is saying that there *can be* aesthetic judgments that no one is prevented from making merely because he or she belongs to one culture rather than another. He is not saying that everyone *must* agree about the attribution of aesthetic properties. Rather, he is saying that it is possible that there *can be* aesthetic properties about which people may agree, regardless of what they believe or know otherwise. In an age of increased interaction between cultures, this cosmopolitan view may be the decisive reason to give priority to the enjoyments of pure forms.

CONCLUSION

The central problem of architectural thinking today is that it seriously lags behind developments in other fields. It relies on psychological and philosophical assumptions that have lost their credibility
in the disciplines they originated from decades ago. In every society
and every culture, thinking about architecture is part of and inseparable from the wider worldview that is credible in the given context.
Nobody needs an understanding of architecture based on premises
that are not credible. Ever since the Renaissance, the most significant
revolutions in architectural theory have been the results of changes
in philosophically and scientifically credible worldviews to which the
discipline had to adjust. Renaissance faith in the harmonic structure
of the universe was shuttered with the collapse of the astronomical
credibility of the geocentric system; this led, in the seventeenth century, to the famous French debate between ancients and moderns.
Similarly, one needs a social context in which the Hegelian understanding of history is well known and accepted in order to argue credibly that, by the will of Zeitgeist, a certain architectural style is appropriate for the twentieth century—as modernists successfully argued
in their time. Or, you need an intellectual environment in which the
ideas of French thinkers such as Derrida or Deleuze are reasonably
well known in order to convincingly propose them as theoretically
significant for the understanding of architecture, as was the case in
the 1980s.

The current situation, in which our understanding of architecture is still hugely dominated by the obsolete dogmas that vision is
inseparable from conceptual thinking, that all thinking is verbal, that
everything is text, that architecture is an art imbued with meanings,
and so on, cannot last. The understanding of human visuality has

changed immensely in the past twenty years, and the understanding of architecture will have to change with it. One can only hope that, once liberated from the need to fabricate stories in order to justify their designs, architects will use this new freedom for the best of our living environment.

NOTES

PREFACE

1. Arnheim, *Dynamics of Architectural Form*, 2.

INTRODUCTION

1. Obviously, these paradigms are rooted in a large body of scholarly works; interpretations and approaches that are not strictly based on the assumption of the primacy of language are also possible. This book may sound critical of the existing "phenomenological" tradition in architectural theory, but it is possible to imagine (phenomenological) approaches that postulate nondiscursive phenomenological "feels" that precede conceptualization and that are perfectly compatible with the formalist viewpoint proposed in this book. (I am indebted to the anonymous reviewer of the book for this observation.) Similarly, in his *Parages* Derrida does actually say that it was not his intention to extend the notion of text "to a whole extra-textual realm" (111). (I am indebted to Kevin J. Hart for drawing my attention to this section.) Obviously, one could respond that if (as Derrida famously claimed) there is nothing outside text, then it is unclear how there can be an "extra-textual realm." In any case, it is not the task of this book to try to provide a consistent interpretation of Derrida's philosophy—arguably an impossible task anyhow.

2. See, e.g., Kanizsa's "Seeing and Thinking." Marr's and Pylyshyn's views are discussed extensively later in the book.

3. Marr, *Vision*. A good summary is in Hatfield, *Perception and Cognition*, 102–3.

4. Noë and Thompson, *Vision and Mind*, 2–3. For Noë's view, see his *Action in Perception*. See also Ned Block's criticism in his review of *Action in Perception*.

5. Psychological research on visual imagery has been a fast-growing field for the past four decades and there exists an immense bibliography on the topic. The classic collection of essays is Block, *Imagery*. See also Eilan, McCarthy, and Brewer, *Spatial Representation*; and Tye, *The Imagery Debate*.

6. Since the late 1990s a substantial body of research has endeavored to specify the processes in the brain that enable human aesthetic reaction. Much

of this research concentrates on the explanation of the processes of recognition in human interaction with artworks. A good introduction to this research can be found in Ramachadran and Hirstein's "The Science of Art"; Freedberg's "Empathy, Movement and Emotion"; and Kesner's "Gombrich and the Problem of Relativity of Vision." More specifically, in relation to architecture, see Mallgrave, *Architect's Brain*.

1 ARCHITECTURE: FORM OR STORY

1. The studio situation I am presenting here is far from being fictional. If one looks through the official documents of architectural educational institutions one can easily find statements that align with the positions of the professors in this description. A recent evaluation document in a New Zealand architecture school thus recommends that "students who do not clearly establish an architectural position/theoretical context for their design proposition should not pass the course."

2. See, e.g., Arnheim, *Dynamics of Architectural Form*, 207–8.

3. "Seeing as" here should not be confused with Wittgenstein's position; see Nyírí, "Image and Metaphor."

4. Wartofsky, *Models*, 188–210, esp. 195.

5. Blunck, *Duchamps Präzionsoptik*, 13–36.

6. See Mitrović, "Intellectual History," for a general methodological discussion of this view; and "Ruminations on the Dark Side," for its history in German art history of the 1920s.

7. Before World War II, the idea that perception is predetermined by membership in a group was distinctly part of German right-wing thinking. Rothacker, *Zur Genealogie*, 44–48, esp. 44.

8. Frey, *Kunstwissenschaftliche Grundfragen*, 33.

9. Bruner and Goodman, "Value and Need."

10. Bruner and Postman, "On the Perception of Incongruity."

11. Gordon, "Gombrich and the Psychology of Visual Perception," 63.

12. Norberg-Schulz, *Intentions in Architecture*, 37.

13. Ibid., 156.

14. Ibid., 124–25.

15. See Mitrović, "A Defence of Light," appendix, for a survey of Gombrich's use of the phrase.

16. Gombrich, *Art and Illusion*, 301.

17. Gombrich, "Image and Code," 286.

18. Popper, *Objective Knowledge*, 61–62, 341–46. See also Gombrich, *Art and Illusion*, 28.

19. See Mitrović, "A Defence of Light," for a survey of these debates.

20. Gombrich, *Art and Illusion*, 363.

21. See Mitrović, "A Defence of Light," for an analysis of Gombrich's response to this problem.

22. In his article "Ambiguities of Representation," Krieger described how Gombrich's book "radically undermined the terms which had controlled discussions of how art represented 'reality.'" Gombrich, who hated the antirealist appropriations of his book, responded with irritation that "this school of criticism . . . had apparently convinced themselves that the book [*Art and Illusion*] lent support to an aesthetics in which the notions of reality and nature had no place." The proponents of this "school," he complained, attributed to him the view "that all that remained were different systems of conventional signs which were made to stand for an unknowable reality" (Gombrich, "Representation and Misrepresentation," 195).

23. See Mitrović, "Defence of Light," for a discussion of such positions in art history.

24. Gombrich's book came out in the same year as W. V. O. Quine's *Word and Object* and Hans Georg Gadamer's *Truth and Method*, eight years before Goodman's *Languages of Art*, and two years before Thomas Kuhn's *Structure of Scientific Revolutions*. These are only some of the most prominent contributors to the rise of cultural relativism in the 1960s.

25. Herder, *Abhandlung*, 85–86. For a historical survey of the view that all thinking is verbal, see Losonsky, *Linguistic Turns*.

26. See n. 1 of the introduction for the interpretative approaches to Derrida that do not postulate the primacy of language.

2   THE EYE IS INNOCENT, BUT THE BRAIN CAN BE A LIAR

1. See Hershenson, *Visual Space Perception*, 29–73, for a general description of binocular vision. Also Churchland, "A Feedforward Network."

2. Similar phenomena can be studied in the cases of patients with lesions in certain parts of the brain's visual cortex—they often produce a blind area, a scotoma, in the visual field. Such patients do not see empty field, but the brain "fills in" that part of the visual field. In their article "Filling In," Churchland

and Ramachandran described the visual perception of some patients who suffered from this problem (143–46). The patients did not experience the scotoma as a gap or a hole in the visual field, although they were aware of the defects in their visual perception. What they noticed was occasionally false filling in; also, they failed to perceive small components of objects. One subject thus reported that he once entered by mistake the women's restroom instead of men's, because "wo" in the word "woman" fell on the scotoma.

3. Dennett, *Conscious Explained,* 356.

4. Churchland and Ramachandran, "Filling In."

5. Ibid., 135–36.

6. See McConkie and Zola, "Is Visual Information Integrated?"; and McConkie, "On the Role of and Control of Eye Movements."

7. For the history of the view that all thinking is verbal, see Losonsky, *Linguistic Turns.*

8. Quine thus says that "there is in principle no separating language from the rest of the world. . . . It is not clear even in principle that it makes sense to think of words and syntax as varying from language to language while the content stays fixed" (*From a Logical Point of View,* 61). Similarly, see Harman, *Reasoning, Meaning and Mind* 166–82, 183–91; and Dummett, *Seas of Language,* 94–105.

9. See Losinsky, *Linguistic Turns.*

10. "The Parthenon is visible; the Parthenon-idea is invisible. We cannot imagine two things more unlike, and less liable to confusion, than the Parthenon and the Parthenon idea" (Quine, *From a Logical Point of View,* 2).

11. For a summary of arguments about translation, see Mitrović, "Intentionalism, Intentionality."

12. See Bermúdez, *Thinking without Words.*

13. There exists a vast philosophical literature about concepts. Good summaries are by Ray, "Concepts"; and by Margolis and Laurence in their introduction, "Concepts and Cognitive Science," to their *Concepts,* 3–82.

14. Margolis and Lawrence, *Concepts,* 10. See also Ray, "Concepts and Stereotypes," 280.

15. Some important arguments against the position that all thinking is verbal derive precisely from that fact that thoughts can be expressed using different words (sentences) in different languages, while the correspondence of words (sentences) is not one-to-one. The view that all thinking is verbal con-

sequently ends up in serious problems when it comes to explaining translation between different languages. See Mitrović, "Intentionalism, Intentionality," for a description of these difficulties.

16. See, similarly, Smith and Klein, "Concept Systems and Ontologies."

17. But it can also be temporal, as is the case with an record player reading grooves from a LP record.

3   PERSPECTIVE AND ITS DISCONTENTS

1. Panofsky, "Perspektive."

2. What I present here is merely a simplified discussion of the problem. There exists a huge psychological literature about the ways changes in the vantage point affect the perception of perspectival drawings. See the comprehensive discussion of the problem in Todorović, "Geometric and Perceptual Effects." This article also includes an extensive bibliography pertaining to the debate.

3. The errors remained unnoticed for more than a decade, until Carrier published his criticism of Goodman's errors in 1980 ("Perspective as a Convention"). An important analysis of Goodman's errors is in Kubovy, *The Psychology of Perspective*, 122–26. See also Mitrović, "Nelson Goodman's Arguments."

4. Goodman, *Languages of Art*, 35–37.

5. Ibid., 38.

6. See Hochberg and Brooks, "Pictorial Recognition"; and also Kennedy, *A Psychology of Picture Perception*, 56.

7. A good summary of this research is in Dirks and Gibson, "Infants' Perception."

8. Ibid. See also DeLoache, Strauss, and Maynard, "Picture Perception in Infancy."

9. Holway and Boring, "Determinants of Apparent Visual Size," 21.

10. Hershenson, *Visual Space Perception*, 118.

11. Massaro, "Perception of Rotated Shapes," 420. See, similarly, Rock and McDermott, "Perception of Visual Angle," 119: "perceptual constancies have in common that phenomenal experience is more in accord with the external object than with the proximal stimulus or at least with that aspect of the proximal stimulus considered most relevant." In other words, size is experienced in objective terms; the specific image size is not directly available to experience.

12. Pizlo, "A Theory of Shape Constancy," 1637. Pizlo's article contains a

valuable historical survey of the four most significant approaches to the problem of constancies.

13. Thouless, "Phenomenal Regression," 339.

14. See, e.g., Gordon, "Gombrich," 62.

15. Doesschate, *Perspective*, 74.

16. See, e.g., Köhler, *Gestalt Psychology*, 44. The same example is repeated
by Gombrich in "Western Art."

17. Thouless, "Phenomenal Regression," 339. See also Thouless's later article "Perceptual Constancy."

18. Thouless, "Phenomenal Regression," 339. Similarly, Köhler, *Gestalt Psychology*, 45. Epstein's introduction to his *Stability* provides a good historical
survey of psychological theories of constancies. Epstein cites William James,
Principles of Psychology (New York: Holt, 1890), 180: "As I look along the dining
table I overlook the fact that the farther plates and glasses *feel* so much smaller
than my own, for I *know* that they are all equal in size; and the feeling of them,
which is a present sensation, is eclipsed in the glare of the knowledge, which
is a merely imagined one" (10).

19. Köhler, *Gestalt Psychology*, 50; Rock, "Unconscious Inference," 347.

20. For this argument, see Carlson, "Instructions," 218.

21. Köhler, *Gestalt Psychology*, 43.

22. Ibid., 44.

23. For a discussion of various implications of Gestalt psychology for architecture and the visual arts, see Arnheim, *Art and Visual Perception, Dynamics of
Architectural Form*, and *Visual Thinking*; and Verstegen, *Arnheim, Gestalt and Art*.

24. For a summary of Köhler's arguments, see his *Gestalt Psychology*; also
Epstein's introduction to his *Stability*.

25. Thouless, "Phenomenal Regression." In another of Thouless's experiments a circular white disc was presented to subjects at various distances
while, at the same time, the subjects could control, using an adjustable dia-
phragm in the lantern, the radius of a white light circle thrown at five meters
distance from the subject. The subject was asked to adjust the circle cast by the
lantern for each position of the white disk until it appeared equal to the disk.
The changes of the perceived size of the disk would have to be proportional to
the distance of the white circle if they followed the laws of perspective; if they
followed the principle of constancies, they would remain the same. However,
it turned out that the apparent size of the disk never remained constant when

distance changed, but it also did not change as rapidly as the laws of perspective would require. Ibid., 354.

26. Holway and Boring, "Determinants of Apparent Visual Size." See also Gilinsky, "The Effect of Attitude," 173, for a summary of these experiments.

27. Leibowitz and Bourne, "Time and Intensity."

28. Epstein, Hatfield, and Muise, "Perceived Shape."

29. See Carlson, "Instructions," 236. Similarly, Gilinsky, "The Effect of Attitude."

30. Hershenson, *Visual Space Perception*, 116.

31. Ibid., 116. But later he describes continuous perspective transformations that result from a movement around the object and directly denies constancies: "A stationary surface at a slant to a viewer projects onto the proximal stimulus as a perspective transformation of the outline shape of the surface. When a viewer moves around the stationary surface, or when the distal surface is in motion, there is a continuous change of the perspective transformation in the proximal stimulus" (154). Note that this is only about the proximal stimulus.

32. Rock and McDermott, "Perception of Visual Angle," 119. See also Rock, "In Defense of Unconscious Inference."

33. Rock and McDermott, "Perception of Visual Angle," 132. Similarly, Slomann, in "Perception of Size," disagrees with the "orthodox" view of constancies formulated as follows: "It is the familiar, ordinary scene of daily life, in which . . . the book across the room looks as big as the book lying in front of you"; and which another psychologist stated as, "This proves to be the case for all things within the so-called near space, which with the observer as centre has a radius of about 12 to 15 meters. All things within this area are seen with their real, constant sizes" (102). Slomann says that he perceives that objects decrease slightly in perceived size when the distance from the eyes increases, and there is no sudden change in the rate of diminishing with increasing distance when this becomes greater than twelve to fifteen meters.

34. Ludwig, "Explaining Why," 50. Also, Bruner and Goodman, "Value and Need," 35; and Rock and McDermott, "Perception of Visual Angle," 132. It has also been demonstrated that the tendency to perceive constancy is inverse to the intelligence of subjects—i.e., more-intelligent subjects tend to perceive perspectively. Leibowitz et al., "Intelligence Level as a Variable."

35. Gombrich, "Mirror and the Map," 193; and "Western Art," 22–23.

36. In other words, if occlusion is properly perceived, our visual perception must follow the geometry of light rays. Consequently, it must be organized according to the laws of perspective. See Gombrich, "Mirror and the Map," 202.

37. Todorović, "Constancies and Illusions," 125.

4   PERCEIVING AND THINKING ABOUT SPACE

1. Marr, *Vision*.

2. For a description of these experiments, see Ittelson, *Ames Demonstrations*.

3. Goodman, *Languages of Art*.

4. For Gombrich's discussions of this problem, see his essay "Mirror and the Map," 191; and "Western Art," 16–17. In the former essay Gombrich discussed but was still hesitant to endorse the explanation that our expectations organize our perspectival visual experience; in the latter essay he adopted this explanation.

5. Hoffman's entire book *Visual Intelligence* is dedicated to surveying these "rules" as he calls them. For a summary, see Pylyshyn, *Seeing and Visualizing*, 107. Similar rules were also described by Perkins, "Cubic Corners." A good summary of Perkins's rules is in Kubovy, *Psychology of Perspective*, 98–103.

6. Marr, *Vision*, 37; see 295 for 3-D models.

7. Luneburg, *Mathematical Analysis*; and "The Metric."

8. A good summary of these attempts in the history of modernist architecture is in Tepavčević, *Uticaj*, 65–76.

9. For summaries of these attempts, see French, *Geometry of Vision*, 74–116; and Wagner, *Geometries of Visual Space*, 30–49.

10. Wagner, *Geometries of Visual Space*, ix–x.

11. Ibid., 3–4.

12. Perky, "An Experimental Study of Imagination." However, later experiments have not fully confirmed Perky's results. See Segal and Nathan, "The Perky Effect"; and Segal, "Assimilation of a Stimulus."

13. The classic article describing these experiments is Shepard and Metzler, "Mental Rotation." A good general summary of these experiments is in Eysenck and Keane, *Cognitive Psychology*, 203–32; and Brown and Herrnstein, "Icons and Images." For a summary of the form of the debates about mental visual imagination in the 1970s, see Cohen, "Visual Imagery in Thought."

14. Shepard and Metzler, "Mental Rotation."

15. Hollard and Delius, "Rotational Invariance."

16. Paivio, "Language and Knowledge of the World."

17. "People often take a lively interest in a controversy in physics or biology or astronomy without feeling the need to take sides, and indeed without deeming themselves equipped to have an opinion worth promoting, but everyone, it seems, has a fiercely confident opinion about the nature and existence of mental images. This manifests itself in remarkable ways: in unhesitating predictions of the results of novel psychological experiments, in flat disbelief in the integrity of recalcitrant experiments, in gleeful citation of 'supporting' experimental evidence, coupled with bland imperviousness to contrary evidence. Since this relatively uninformed or pretheoretical partisanship comes in both varieties—iconophile and iconophobe—one breathtakingly simple explanation of the phenomenon, and one that is often proposed, is that in fact some people do have mental images and others don't" (Dennett, "Two Approaches to Mental Images," 88).

18. Dennett, "The Nature of Images."

19. Fodor, "Imaginistic Representation."

20. Kosslyn, "On the Demystification of Mental Imagery."

21. See Michael Tye, *The Imagery Debate*, 35–60, for a discussion of Kosslyn's position.

22. Pylyshyn, "The Imagery Debate."

23. Kosslyn, "Medium and the Message."

24. Pallasmaa, "An Architecture of the Seven Senses," 31.

25. Ibid., 32.

26. In psychology, there exists an extensive debate about the contribution of individual senses to the formulation of the idea of space, including the view that our comprehension of space is fundamentally driven by the sense of sight. This may be the case even when it comes to congenitally blind people, who may be relying on visual imagination in understanding spatial relationships. It is far from clear which senses constitute our experience of spatiality, what is the contribution of individual senses to this experience, and so on. Do *different* senses constitute the *same* spatial experience? Do they describe the *same* space? Karlsson, "The Experience of Spatiality," presents some valuable insights into these questions.

27. See Nagel, "What Is It Like to be a Bat?" for a discussion of the reasons that make the world experience of a bat inaccessible to humans.

28. Pallasmaa, "Hapticity and Time." He makes the same point in *The Eyes of the Skin,* 30. But when he says, in the beginning of the same section, that this is the reason why we have lost spatial experience, one has to wonder how much spatial experience there can be without visuality.

29. Pérez-Gómez presents a comprehensive formulation of the anti-visual approach to architecture in his "Space of Architecture": "Architectural work is therefore articulated as a narrative, 'metaphoric' projection grounded on recollection" (24).

30. Pallasmaa, "Hapticity and Time."

31. "Mental Rotation," *Wikipedia,* http://en.wikipedia.org/wiki/Mental _rotation, accessed 16 May 2011.

32. An important body of research on this topic is being carried out at the University of Novi Sad by Predrag Šidjanin and Radovan Štulić.

33. One should be careful, however, when using the phrase "mental model," because in contemporary psychology the phrase is used for logical, nonvisual, and nonspatial models of thinking. See Johnson-Laird, "Mental Models."

34. Schmarsow, "Essence of Architectural Creation," 286.

5   THE RETURN OF THE VISUAL

1. We have seen above that Norberg-Schulz openly stated that only known things can be properly perceived.

2. A good summary of this research is Bermúdez and Cahen, "Nonconceptual Mental Content." See also Brewer, "Perceptual Experience"; and Byrne, "Perception and Conceptual Content." Raftopoulos's book *Cognition and Perception* provides a particularly useful discussion of the topic in relation to psychological studies on the impenetrability of vision.

3. See Bermúdez and Cahen, "Nonconceptual Mental Content," for a summary of these arguments.

4. For this argument, see Peacocke, "Scenarios, Concepts, and Perception," 111.

5. Crane, "The Waterfall Illusion."

6. Raftopoulos, *Cognition and Perception,* 144.

7. Ibid., 136–37.

8. Pylyshyn, *Things and Places,* provides a comprehensive psychological discussion of the problem and the related research.

9. See Hatfield, *Perception and Cognition,* 5.

10. Marr, *Vision.*

11. Marr did not use the term "late vision"; the phrase is Hatfield's, *Perception and Cognition,* 54.

12. Pylyshyn, "Is Vision Continuous?"

13. Pylyshyn, *Seeing and Visualizing,* 50.

14. Before Pylyshyn, the same argument was formulated by Gregory, "How Do We Interpret Images?" 329.

15. Pylyshyn, *Seeing and Visualizing,* 71.

16. Ibid., 68–70.

17. For Pylyshyn's views on the historical developments in psychology, see his "Is Vision Continuous?" 341–42; and *Seeing and Visualizing,* 49, 83.

18. See Zangwill, *Metaphysics of Beauty.*

19. This interpretation, however, does not correspond exactly to Zangwill's definition of formal properties as presented in *Metaphysics of Beauty,* 83–84. Formal aesthetic properties as he defines them there depend on narrow properties, and the latter include also physical properties, presumably the material a thing is made of.

BIBLIOGRAPHY

Aglioti, Salvatore, Joseph DeSouza, and Melvyn Goodale. "Size-Contrast Illusions Deceive the Eye but Not the Hand." *Current Biology* 5 (1995): 679–85.

Anderson, John. "Arguments Concerning Representations for Mental Imagery." *Psychological Review* 85 (1978): 249–77.

Arnheim, Rudolf. *Art and Visual Perception*. Berkeley: University of California Press, 1974.

———. *The Dynamics of Architectural Form*. Berkeley: University of California Press, 1977.

———. *Visual Thinking*. Berkeley: University of California Press, 1972.

Baghramian, Maria. *Relativism*. London: Routledge, 2004.

Bakoš, Ján. "Introductory: Gombrich's Struggle against Metaphysics." *Human Affairs* 19 (2009): 239–50.

Banks, William. "Assessing Relations between Imagery and Perception." *Journal of Experimental Psychology* 7 (1981): 844–47.

Bartolomeo, Paolo. "The Relationship between Visual Perception and Visual Mental Imagery: A Reappraisal of the Neuropsychological Evidence." *Cortex* 38 (2002): 357–78.

Bermúdez, José. *Thinking without Words*. Oxford: Oxford University Press, 2003.

Bermúdez, José, and Arnon Cahen. "Nonconceptual Mental Content." In *The Stanford Encyclopedia of Philosophy*, Summer 2011 ed., ed. Edward N. Zalta. http://plato.stanford.edu/archives/sum2011/entries/content-nonconceptual/.

Biederman, Irving, and Eric Cooper. "Size Invariance in Visual Object Priming." *Journal of Experimental Psychology* 18 (1992): 121–33.

Blinder, David. "The Controversy over Conventionalism." *Journal of Aesthetics and Art Criticism* 41 (1983): 253–64.

Block, Ned. *Imagery*. Cambridge, Mass.: MIT Press, 1981.

———. Review of *Action in Perception*, by Alva Noë. *Journal of Philosophy* 102 (2005): 259–72.

Blunck, Lars. *Duchamps Präzionsoptik*. Berlin: Verlag Silke Schreber, 2008.

Brewer, Bill. "Perceptual Experience Has Conceptual Content." In *Contemporary Debates in Epistemology*, edited by Matthias Steup and Ernest Sosa, 217–30. Malden, Mass.: Blackwell, 2005.

Brigell, Mitchell, John Uhlarik, and Paul Goldhorn. "Contextual Influences on Judgments of Linear Extent." *Journal of Experimental Psychology* 3 (1977): 105–18.

Brown, Donald. *Human Universals.* Boston: McGraw Hill, 1991.

Brown, Roger, and Richard Herrnstein. "Icons and Images." In Block, *Imagery,* 19–28.

Bruner, Jerome, and Cecile Goodman. "Value and Need as Organizing Factors in Perception." *Journal of Abnormal and Social Psychology* 42 (1947): 33–44.

Bruner, Jerome, and Leon Postman. "On the Perception of Incongruity: A Paradigm." *Journal of Personality* 18 (1949): 206–23.

Bryson, Norman. *Vision and Painting: The Logic of the Gaze.* London: Macmillan, 1985.

Byrne, Alex. "Perception and Conceptual Content." In *Contemporary Debates in Epistemology,* edited by Matthias Steup and Ernest Sosa, 231–50. Malden, Mass.: Blackwell, 2005.

Carlson, V. R. "Instructions and Perceptual Constancy Judgments." In Epstein, *Stability and Constancy,* 217–54.

Carrier, David. "Perspective as a Convention: On the Views of Nelson Goodman and Ernst Gombrich." *Leonardo* 13 (1980): 283–87.

Cheng, Ken. "A Purely Geometric Module in the Rat's Spatial Representation." *Cognition* 23 (1986): 149–78.

Churchland, Paul. "A Feedforward Network for Fast Stereo Vision with Movable Fusion Plane." In *Perception,* edited by Kathleen Akins, 61–88. New York: Oxford University Press, 1996.

Churchland, Paul, and Vilayanur Ramachandran. "Filling In: Why Dennett Is Wrong." In *Perception,* edited by Kathleen Akins, 132–57. New York: Oxford University Press, 1996.

Cohen, Gillian. "Visual Imagery in Thought." *New Literary History* 7 (1976): 513–23.

Crane, Tim. "The Waterfall Illusion." In *Essays on Nonconceptual Content,* edited by York Gunther, 231–35. Cambridge, Mass.: MIT Press, 2003.

Currie, Gregory. "Visual Imagery as the Simulation of Vision." *Mind and Vision* 10 (1995): 25–44.

DeLoache, Judy, Mark Strauss, and Jane Maynard. "Picture Perception in Infancy." *Infant Behavior and Development* 2 (1979): 77–89.

Dennett, Daniel. *Consciousness Explained.* New York: Little, Brown, 1991.

———. "The Nature of Images and the Introspective Trap." In Block, *Imagery*, 51–60.

———. "Two Approaches to Mental Images." In Block, *Imagery*, 87–107.

Derrida, Jacques. *Parages*. Edited by John P. Leavey. Translated by Tom Conley, James Hulbert, John P. Leavey, and Avital Ronell. Stanford: Stanford University Press, 2011.

Dirks, Jean, and Eleanor Gibson. "Infants' Perception of Similarity between Live People and Their Photographs." *Child Development* 48 (1977): 124–30.

Doesschate, Ten. *Perspective: Fundamentals, Controversials, History.* Nieuwkoop: B. De Graaf, 1964.

Dretske, Fred. *Seeing and Knowing.* Chicago: University of Chicago Press, 1969.

Dummett, Michael. *The Seas of Language.* Oxford: Clarendon, 1993.

Eilan, Naomi, Rosaleen McCarthy, and Bill Brewer. *Spatial Representation: Problems in Philosophy and Psychology.* Oxford: Oxford University Press, 1993.

Eisenman, Peter. *Eisenman Inside Out: Selected Writings, 1963–1988.* New Haven: Yale University Press, 2004.

Eissler, Kurt. "Die Gestaltkonstanz der Sehdinge bei Variation der Objekte und ihrer Einwirkungweise auf den Wahrnehmenden." *Archiv für Gestaltpsychologie* 88 (1933): 487–50.

Ellis, Willis. *A Source Book of Gestalt Psychology.* New York: Routledge, 1999.

Epstein, William, ed. *Stability and Constancy in Visual Perception.* New York: John Wiley, 1977.

Epstein, William, Gary Hatfield, and Gerard Muise. "Perceived Shape at a Slant as a Function of Processing Time and Processing Load." *Journal of Experimental Psychology* 3 (1977): 473–83.

Eysenck, Michael, and Mark Keane. *Cognitive Psychology: A Student's Handbook.* Hove, UK: Psychology Press, 1995.

Farah, Marta. "The Neurological Basis of Mental Imagery." *Cognition* 18 (1984): 245–72.

Fish, William. *Philosophy of Perception: Contemporary Introduction.* New York: Routledge, 2010.

Fodor, Jerry. "Imaginistic Representation." In Block, *Imagery*, 63–86.

Freedberg, David. "Empathy, Movement and Emotion." In *Sistemi Emotivi: Artisti contemporanei ta emozione e ragione / Emotional systems: Contemporary Art between Emotion and Reason,* edited by Franziska Nori and Martin Steinhoff, 38–61. Milan: Silvana Editoriale, 2007.

French, Robert. *The Geometry of Vision*. New York: Peter Lang, 1987.

Frey, Dagobert. *Kunstwissenschaftliche Grundfragen: Prolegomena zu einer Kunst-philosophie*. Vienna: R. M. Rohrer Verlag, 1946.

Gilinsky, Alberta. "The Effect of Attitude upon the Perception of Size." *American Journal of Psychology* 68 (1955): 173–92.

Gogel, Walter. "The Organization of Perceived Space." In Rock, *Indirect Perception*, 361–86.

———. "A Theory of Phenomenal Geometry." *Perception and Psychophysics* 48 (1990): 105–23.

Gombrich, Ernst. *Art and Illusion: A Study in the Psychology of Pictorial Representation*. London: Phaidon, 1960.

———. "The Evidence of Images: The Variability of Vision." In *Interpretation: Theory and Practice*, edited by Charles Singleton, 35–68. Baltimore: John Hopkins University Press, 1969.

———. *Ideals and Idols: Essays on Values in History and in Art*. Oxford: Phaidon, 1979.

———. "Illusion and Art." In *Illusion in Nature and Art*, edited by Ernest Gombrich and Richard Gregory, 193–243. New York: Scribner, 1973.

———. *The Image and the Eye*. London: Phaidon, 1982.

———. *Meditations on a Hobby Horse and Other Essays on the Theory of Art*. London and New York: Phaidon, 1963.

———. "Mirror and the Map: Theories of Pictorial Representation." In *The Image and the Eye*, 172–214.

———. *The Preference for the Primitive: Episodes in the History of Western Taste and Art*. New York: Phaidon, 2002.

———. "Representation and Misrepresentation." *Critical Inquiry* 11 (1984): 195–201.

———. *The Sense of Order: A Study in the Psychology of Decorative Art*. Oxford: Phaidon, 1979.

———. *Symbolic Images: Studies in the Art of the Renaissance*. London: Phaidon, 1972.

———. "Western Art and the Perception of Space." In *Space in European Art*, Council of Europe Exhibition, edited by Kokuritsu Seiyo Bijutsukan, 16–28. Tokyo: Yomiuri Shinbunsha, 1987.

———. "The 'What' and the 'How': Perspective Representation and the Phenomenal World." In *Logic and Art: Essays in Honor of Nelson Goodman*, edited by Richard Rudner and Israel Scheffler, 129–49. Indianapolis: Bobbs-Merrill, 1972.

Goodman, Nelson: "Art and Illusion: A Study in the Psychology of Pictorial Representation by E. H. Gombrich." *Journal of Philosophy* 57 (1960): 595–99.

———. *Languages of Art: An Approach to a Theory of Symbols.* Indianapolis: Hackett, 1976.

———. *Ways of Worldmaking.* Indianapolis: Hackett, 1978.

Gordon, Ian. "Gombrich and the Psychology of Visual Perception." In *Gombrich on Art and Psychology,* edited by Richard Woodfield, 60–77. Manchester: Manchester University Press, 1996.

Gregory, Richard. "How Do We Interpret Images?" In *Images and Understanding,* edited by Horace Barolow, Colin Blackmore, and Miranda Weston-Smith, 310–30. Cambridge: Cambridge University Press, 1990.

Hall, Harrison. "Intentionality and World: Division I of *Being and Time.*" In *The Cambridge Companion to Heidegger,* edited by Charles Guignon, 122–40. Cambridge: Cambridge University Press, 1994.

Hamlyn, David. *Sensation and Perception: A History of the Philosophy of Perception.* New York: Humanities Press, 1961.

Hansen, Robert. "The Curving World: Hyperbolic Linear Perspective." *Journal of Aesthetics and Art Criticism* 32 (1973): 147–61.

Harman, Gilbert. *Reasoning, Meaning and Mind.* Oxford: Clarendon Press, 2005.

Hatfield, Gary. *Perception and Cognition: Essays in the Philosophy of Psychology.* Oxford: Clarendon, 2009.

Heidegger, Martin. *Holzwege.* Frankfurt: Klostermann, 1952.

———. *Sein und Zeit.* Tübingen: Max Niemeyer Verlag, 1993.

Herder, Johann Gottfried. *Abhandlung über den Ursprung der Sprache.* Stuttgart: Phillip Reclam, 1966.

Hershenson, Maurice. *Visual Space Perception.* Cambridge, Mass.: MIT Press, 1999.

Hochberg, Julian, and Virginia Brooks. "Pictorial Recognition as an Unlearned Ability: A Study of One Child's Performance." *American Journal of Psychology* 75 (1962): 624–28.

Hochberg, Julian, and Mary Peterson. "Necessary Considerations for a Theory of Form Perception: A Theoretical and Empirical Reply to Boselie and Leeuwenberg (1986)." *Perception* 18 (1989): 115–19.

Hoffman, Donald. *Visual Intelligence.* New York: Norton, 1998.

Hollard, Valerie, and Juan Delius. "Rotational Invariance in Visual Pattern Recognition by Pigeons and Humans." *Science* 218 (1982): 804–6.

Holway, Alfred, and Edwin Boring. "Determinants of Apparent Visual Size with Distance Variant." *American Journal of Psychology* 54 (1941): 21–37.

Indow, Tarow. "An Approach to Geometry of Visual Space." *Journal of Mathematical Psychology* 26 (1982): 204–36.

———. "A Critical Review of Luneberg's Model." *Psychological Review* 98 (1991): 430–53.

Ittelson, William. *The Ames Demonstrations.* New York: Hafner, 1968.

Johnson-Laird, Philip. "Mental Models in Cognitive Science." *Cognitive Science* 4 (1980): 71–115.

Kanizsa, Gaetano. "Seeing and Thinking." *Acta Psychologica* 59 (1985): 23–33.

Karlsson, Gunnar. "The Experience of Spatiality for Congenitally Blind People: A Phenomenological-Psychological Study." *Human Studies* 19 (1996): 303–30.

Kennedy, John. "Haptic Pictures." *Papers in Language Use and Language Function* 13 (1980): 1–97.

———. *A Psychology of Picture Perception.* San Francisco: Jossey-Bass, 1974.

Kesner, Ladislav. "Gombrich and the Problem of the Relativity of Vision." *Human Affairs* 19 (2009): 266–73.

Koenderink, Jan. "Optic Flow." *Vision Research* 26 (1986): 161–80.

Koenderink, Jan, Andrea van Doorn, and Joseph Lapin. "Direct Measurement of the Curvature of Visual Space." *Perception* 29 (2000): 69–79.

Köhler, Wolfgang. *Gestalt Psychology.* New York: New American Library, 1947.

Kosslyn, Stephen Michael. *Ghosts in the Mind's Machine: Creating and Using Images in the Brain.* New York: Norton, 1983.

———. "The Medium and the Message in Mental Imagery." In Block, *Imagery,* 207–44.

———. "On the Demystification of Mental Imagery." In Block, *Imagery,* 131–50.

Krieger, Murray. "The Ambiguities of Representation and Illusion: An E. H. Gombrich Retrospective." *Critical Inquiry* 11 (1984): 181–95.

Kubovy, Michael. *The Psychology of Perspective and Renaissance Art.* Cambridge: Cambridge University Press, 1986.

Langdon, J. "The Perception of a Changing Shape." *Quarterly Journal of Experimental Psychology* 3 (1951): 157–65.

Leibowitz, H., and L. E. Bourne. "Time and Intensity as Determiners of Perceived Shape." *Journal of Experimental Psychology* 51 (1956): 277–81.

Leibowitz, H., I. Waskow, N. Loeffler, and F. Glaser. "Intelligence Level as a Variable in the Perception of Shape." *Quarterly Journal of Experimental Psychology* 11 (1959): 108–12.

Losonsky, Michael. *Linguistic Turns in Modern Philosophy*. New York: Cambridge University Press, 2006.

Ludwig, Kirk. "Explaining Why Things Look the Way They Do." In *Perception,* edited by Kathleen Akins, 18–60. New York: Oxford University Press, 1996.

Luneburg, Rudolf. *Mathematical Analysis of Binocular Vision*. Princeton: Princeton University Press, 1947.

———. "The Metric of Binocular Visual Space." *Journal of the Optical Society of America* 40 (1950): 627–42.

Mallgrave, Harry Francis. *The Architect's Brain: Neuroscience, Creativity and Architecture*. Chichester: John Wiley and Sons, 2010.

Margolis, Eric, and Stephen Laurence. *Concepts: Core Readings*. Cambridge, Mass.: MIT Press, 1999.

Marr, David. *Vision: A Computational Investigation into the Human Representation and Processing of Visual Information*. San Francisco: W. H. Freeman, 1982.

Massaro, Dominic. "The Perception of Rotated Shapes: A Process Analysis of Shape Constancy." *Perception and Psychophysics* 13 (1973): 413–22.

McConkie, George. "On the Role of and Control of Eye Movements in Reading." In *Processing of Visual Language,* edited by Paul Kolers, Ernst Merald, and Herman Bouma, 37–48. New York: Plenum Press, 1979.

McConkie, George, and David Zola. "Is Visual Information Integrated across Successive Fixations in Reading?" *Perception and Psychophysics* 25 (1979): 221–24.

McCready, Don. "On Size, Distance, and Visual Angle Perception." *Perception and Psychophysics* 37 (1985): 323–34.

Mitrović, Branko. "Architectural Formalism and the Demise of the Linguistic Turn." *Log* 17 (2009): 17–25.

———. "A Defence of Light: Ernst Gombrich, the Innocent Eye and Seeing in Perspective." *Journal of Art Historiography* 3 (2010). http://arthistoriography .files.wordpress.com/2011/02/media_183173_en.pdf.

———. "Humanist Art History and Its Enemies: Erwin Panofsky on the Individualism-Collectivism Debate." *Konsthistorisk Tidskrift* 78 (2009): 57–76.

———. "Intellectual History, Inconceivability and Methodological Holism." *History and Theory* 46 (2007): 29–47.

———. "Intentionalism, Intentionality and Reporting Beliefs." *History and Theory* 48 (2009): 180–98.

———. "Nelson Goodman's Arguments against Perspective." Forthcoming in *Nexus Network Journal*.

———. "Ruminations on the Dark Side: History of Art as Rage and Denials." *Journal of Art Historiography* 1 (2009). http://arthistoriography.files.word press.com/2011/02/media_139139_en.pdf.

Nagel, Thomas. "What Is It Like to Be a Bat?" *Philosophical Review* 83 (1974): 435–50.

Noë, Alva. *Action in Perception*. Cambridge, Mass.: MIT Press, 2005.

Noë, Alva, and Evan Thompson. *Vision and Mind*. Cambridge, Mass.: MIT Press, 2002.

Norberg-Schulz, Christian. *Intentions in Architecture*. 2nd ed. Oslo: Universitetsforlaget, 1966.

Nyíri, Kristóf. "Image and Metaphor in the Philosophy of Wittgenstein." In *Image and Imaging in Philosophy, Science and the Arts*, edited by Richard Heinrich, Elisabeth Nemeth, Wolfram Pichler, and David Wagner, 1:109–29. Frankfurt: Ontos Verlag, 2011.

Ono, Hiroshi, Brian Rogers, Massao Ohmi, and Mika Ono. "Dynamic Occlusion and Motion Parallax in Depth Perception." *Perception* 17 (1988): 255–66.

Ono, Mika, José Rivest, and Hiroshi Ono. "Depth Perception as a Function of Motion Parallax and Absolute-Distance Information." *Journal of Experimental Psychology: Human Perception and Performance* 12 (1986): 331–37.

Paivio, Allan. "Language and Knowledge of the World." *Educational Researcher* 3 (1974): 5–12.

Pallasmaa, Juhani. "An Architecture of the Seven Senses." In *Questions of Perception: Phenomenology of Architecture*, edited by Steven Hall, Alberto Perez-Gomez, and Juhani Pallasmaa, 27–38. San Francisco: William Stout, 2007.

———. *The Eyes of the Skin*. Chichester: John Wiley and Sons, 2005.

———. "Hapticity and Time." 1999 RIBA Discourse Lecture. http://iris.nyit .edu/~rcody/Thesis/Readings/Pallasmaa%20–20Hapticity%20and%20 Time.pdf, accessed 19 May 2011.

Panofsky, Erwin. "Die Perspektive als 'symbolische Form.'" Leipzig: Bibliothek Warburg, 1927.

Peacocke, Christopher. "Scenarios, Concepts, and Perception." In *Essays on Nonconceptual Content*, edited by York Gunther, 107–32. Cambridge, Mass.: MIT Press, 2003.

Perez-Gomez, Alberto. "The Space of Architecture: Meaning as Presence and Representation." In *Questions of Perception: Phenomenology of Architecture*, edited by Steven Hall, Alberto Perez-Gomez, and Juhani Pallasmaa, 7–26. San Francisco: William Stout, 2007.

Perkins, David. "Cubic Corners, Oblique Views of Pictures, the Perception of Line Drawings of Simple Space Forms: Geometry and the Perception of Pictures: Three Studies." Technical Report No. 5. http://www.eric.ed .gov:80/ERICWebPortal/search/detailmini.jsp?_nfpb=true&_&ERICExt Search_SearchValue_0=ED114328&ERICExtSearch_SearchType_0=no& accno=ED114328, accessed 28 October 2011.

Perky, Cheves West. "An Experimental Study of Imagination." *American Journal of Psychology* 21 (1910): 422–52.

Pinker, Steven. *The Blank Slate: The Modern Denial of Human Nature.* London: Allen Lane, 2002.

Pizlo, Zygmunt. "A Theory of Shape Constancy Based on Perspective Invariants." *Visual Research* 34 (1994): 1637–58.

Popper, Karl. *Objective Knowledge; an Evolutionary Approach.* Oxford: Clarendon, 1972.

Pylyshyn, Zenon. "The Imagery Debate: Analog Media versus Tacit Knowledge." In Block, *Imagery*, 151–204.

———. "Is Vision Continuous with Cognition? The Case for Cognitive Impenetrability of Visual Perception." *Behavioural and Brain Sciences* 22 (1999): 341–423.

———. *Seeing and Visualizing: It's Not What You Think.* Cambridge, Mass.: MIT Press, 2006.

———. *Things and Places: How the Mind Connects with the World.* Cambridge, Mass.: MIT Press, 2007.

Quine, Willard van Orman. *From a Logical Point of View.* New York: Harper and Row, 1961.

Raftopoulos, Athanassios. *Cognition and Perception: How Do Psychology and Neural Science Inform Philosophy?* Cambridge, Mass.: MIT Press, 2009.

Ramachandran, Vilayanur. "Perception of Shape from Shading." *Nature* 331 (1988): 163–66.

Ramachadran, Vilayanur, and William Hirstein. "The Science of Art: A Neurological Theory of Aesthetic Experience." *Journal of Consciousness Studies* 6/7 (1999): 15–51.

Ray, George. "Concepts." In *A Companion to the Philosophy of Mind,* edited by Samuel Gutenplan, 185–93. Oxford: Blackwell, 1994.

———. "Concepts and Stereotypes." In Margolis and Laurence, *Concepts,* 279–99.

Rock, Irvin. Rock, "In Defense of Unconscious Inference." In Epstein, *Stability and Constancy,* 321–72.

———, ed. *Indirect Perception.* Cambridge, Mass.: MIT Press, 1997.

Rock, Irvin, and William McDermott. "The Perception of Visual Angle." *Acta Psychologica* 22 (1964): 119–34.

Rothacker, Erich. *Zur Genealogie des menschlichen Bewusstseins.* Bonn: H. Bouvier u. Co. Verlag, 1966.

Runeson, S. "The Distorted Room Illusion." *Journal of Experimental Psychology* 14 (1988): 295–304.

Sacks, Oliver. *The Man Who Mistook His Wife for a Hat and Other Clinical Tales.* New York: Touchstone, 1998.

Schmarsow, August. "The Essence of Architectural Creation." In *Empathy, Form, and Space: Problems in German Aesthetics, 1873–1893,* by Robert Vischer et al. With an introduction and translated by Harry Francis Mallgrave and Elefterios Ikonomou, 281–98. Santa Monica: Getty Center for the History of Art and the Humanities, 1994.

Searle, John. *Intentionality.* Cambridge: Cambridge University Press, 1983.

Segal, Sydney. "Assimilation of a Stimulus in the Construction of an Image: The Perky Effect Revisited." In *The Function and Nature of Imagery,* edited by Peter Sheehan, 203–30. New York: Academic Press 1972.

Segal, Sydney, and Shifra Nathan. "The Perky Effect: Incorporation of an External Stimulus into Imagery Experience under Placebo and Control Conditions." *Perceptual and Motor Skills* 18 (1964): 385–95.

Shepard, Roger, and Jacqueline Metzler. "Mental Rotation of Three-Dimensional Objects." *Science* 141 (1971): 701–3.

Slomann, Aage. "Perception of Size: Some Remarks on Size as a Primary Quality and 'Size Constancy.'" *Inquiry* 11 (1968): 101–13.

Smith, Barry, and Gunnar Klein. "Concept Systems and Ontologies." *Transactions of the Japanese Society for Artificial Intelligence* 25 (2010): 433–41.

Suppes, Patrick. "Is Visual Space Euclidean?" *Synthese* 35 (1977): 397–421.

Tepavčević, Bojan. "Uticaj geometrijske reprezentacije prostora na savremenu arhitekturu." Ph.D. dissertation, University of Novi Sad, 2010.

Thouless, Robert. "Perceptual Constancy or Perceptual Compromise." *Australian Journal of Psychology* 24 (1972): 133–40.

———. "Phenomenal Regression to the Real Object." *British Journal of Psychology* 21 (1931): 339–59.

Todorović, Dejan. "Constancies and Illusions in Visual Perception." *Psihologija* 35 (2002): 125–207.

———. "The Effect of the Observer Vantage Point on Perceived Distortions in Linear Perspective Images." *Attention, Perception, Psychophysics* 71 (2009): 183–93.

———. "Geometric and Perceptual Effects of the Location of the Observer Vantage Point for Linear-Perspective Images." *Perception* 34 (2005): 521–44.

———. "Is Pictorial Perception Robust? The Effect of the Observer Vantage Point on the Perceived Depth Structure of Linear Perspective Images." *Perception* 37 (2008): 106–25.

Topper, David. "On the Fidelity of Pictures." *Philosophia* 14 (1984): 187–97.

———. "Perspectives on Perspective: Gombrich and His Critics." In *Gombrich on Art and Psychology*, edited by Richard Woodfield, 78–99. Manchester: Manchester University Press, 1996.

Toye, Richard. "The Effect of Viewing Position on the Perceived Layout of Space." *Perception and Psychophysics* 40 (1986): 85–92.

Tye, Michael. *The Imagery Debate.* Cambridge, Mass.: MIT Press, 1991.

Verstegen, Ian. "Arnheim and Gombrich in Social Scientific Perspective." *Journal for the Theory of Social Behaviour* 34 (2004): 91–102.

———. *Arnheim, Gestalt, and Art: A Psychological Theory.* Vienna and New York: Springer, 2005.

Wagner, Mark. *Geometries of Visual Space.* Mahwah, N.J.: Erlbaum, 2006.

———. "The Metric of Visual Space." *Perception of Psychophysics* 38 (1985): 483–95.

Walton, Kendall. "Categories of Art." *Philosophical Review* 79 (1970): 334–67.

Wartofsky, Marx. *Models: Representation and the Scientific Understanding.* Dordrecht: D. Reidel, 1979.

Woodfield, Richard. "Ernst Gombrich and the Idea of Human Nature." *Human Affairs* 13 (2003): 163–70.

———. "Gombrich, Formalism and the Description of Works of Art." *British Journal of Aesthetics* 34 (1994): 134–45.

———. "Gombrich on Language and Meaning." *British Journal of Aesthetics* 25 (1985): 389–93.

———. "Gombrich on Perception and Mental Set." *Nordisk Estetisk Tidskrift* 16 (1996): 65–75.

———. "Words and Pictures." *British Journal of Aesthetics* 26 (1986): 357–70.

Zangwill, Nick. *The Metaphysics of Beauty.* Ithaca: Cornell University Press, 2001.

INDEX

www.ingramcontent.com/pod-product-compliance
Lightning Source LLC
Chambersburg PA
CBHW020707270326
41928CB00005B/317